ctural Design

Guest-edited by Jan Kaplicky

WILEY-ACADEMY

AD

Architectural Design
Vol 71 No 5 September 2001

ISBN 0-470-84228-8
Profile No 153

Editorial Offices
International House
Ealing Broadway Centre
London W5 5DB
T: +44 (0)20 8326 3800
F: +44 (0)20 8326 3801
E: info@wiley.co.uk

Editor
Helen Castle

Exexcutive Editor
Maggie Toy

Production
Famida Rasheed

Art Director
Christian Küsters ↪ CHK Design

Designer
Owen Peyton Jones ↪ CHK Design

Picture Editor
Famida Rasheed

Advertisement Sales
01243 843272

Photo Credits
AD Architectural Design

Abbreviated positions
b=bottom, c=centre, l=left, r=right, t=top

pp 6, 7, 8, 9, 10, 11 & 12 courtesy Jan Kaplicky; pp 13 & 14(b) © Design Museum/Amando Salas Portugal, Barragán Foundation, Switzerland; p 15 © Michael Halberstadt/Arcaid; p 16(t) courtesy Ron Arad Associates, photo: Perry Hagopian; pp 16(c), 16(br), 17 & 21 © Ron Arad Associates; p 19(b) photo: © Maria Mulas, Milan; p 18 & 19(t) the publishers have made every attempt to trace the original source of these images and contact the copyright holders; p 20(t) © Bieffe SpA; pp 20(tr) & 20(b) courtesy of Kartell, Italy; p 22(t) courtesy Klaus Bode, BDSP Partnership, pp 22(b) & 24(t) © Buro Happold; p 24(b) & 25(t) courtesy Klaus Bode, BDSP Partnership; pp 26– 33 photos courtesy of the Boeing Company; p 34(t) © Steve Pyke & Light Industry; p 34(b) courtesy Bavarian State Library, Munich; p 35 courtesy Anthony d'Offay Gallery, London, © Jeff Koons; p 36(t) courtesy Museum of Modern Art, New York, © Succession Picasso/DACS 2001; p 36(b) courtesy Bridgeman Art Library, © Succesion H Matisse/DACS 2001; p 37(t) courtesy National Gallery of Australia, Canberra, © ARS, NY and DACS, London 2001; p 37(b) © Hunterian Art Gallery, University of Glasgow, Mackintosh Collection; p 38 © courtesy Tony Shafrazi Gallery, New York, © The Estate of Francis Bacon; p 39(t) courtesy Foster and Partners, photo:
Ken Kirkwood; p 39(b) courtesy RIBA Library Photographs Collection, © FLC/ADAGP, Paris and DACS, London 2001; p 40 courtesy Brian Clarke, © Gilbert and George; p 41(t) courtesy Brian Clarke, © David Bailey; p 41(b) courtesy Brian Clarke, © Ralph Gibson; p 42(t) courtesy Brian Clarke, © Richard Hamilton 2001. All Rights Reserved, DACS; p 42(b) courtesy the Brant Foundation, Greenwich, CT, USA, © ADAGP, Paris and DACS, London 2001; p 43 private collection, courtesy Tony Shafrazi Gallery, New York, © The Andy Warhol Foundation for Visual Arts, Inc/ARS, NY and DACS, London 2001; p 44(t) courtesy Peter Cook; p 44(b) and pp 45–9 © Clorindo Testa; p 50 courtesy Kathryn Gustafson, photo: Gordon Spooner; p 50(b) © Kevin Noble, courtesy of Isamu Noguchi Foundation, Inc; p 51(t) © Kathryn Gustafson; p 51(b) courtesy Design Museum, London, © Isamu Noguchi Foundation, Inc, New York; pp 52–7 © Kathryn Gustafson; p 58(t) courtesy Zaha Hadid, © Steve Double; pp 58(b), 59, 60, 68 & 69 © Zaha Hadid; pp 61, 62 & 63 © Iain Borden; pp 64–5 © Adrian Forty; p 66

courtesy Architectural Association Photo Library, © Penny Shefton; p 67(t) © M Blackman/Camera Press Ltd; pp 70–5 © Tony Hunt; p 76 courtesy Anish Kapoor; p 77(t) courtesy Louisiana Museum of Modern Art, Humlebaek, Denmark, © DACS; p 77(b) National Museum of Photography, Film & Television/Science & Society Picture Library; p 78(t) © Michelle Garett/CORBIS; p 78(cl) Bridgeman Art Library; p 78(cr), 78(bl) and 78(br) The Ronald Grant Archive, courtesy 20th-Century Fox; p 79(t) © Museo Thyssen-Bornemisza, Madrid; p 80(b) courtesy Anish Kapoor; p 80(t) courtesy Ramakrishna-Vivekananda Center, New York/ photograph reprinted by permission from THE GOSPEL OF SRI RAMAKRISHNA (complete unabridged edition) as translated into English by Swami Nikhilananda and published by the Ramakrishna-Vivekananda Center of New York, copyright 1942 by Swami Nikhilananda; p 80(b) Photo Scala, Florence; p 81(t) V&A Picture Library; p 81(b) courtesy Devika Singh, © Raghubir Singh; p 82(t) courtesy Anish Kapoor; p 82(b) The Royal Collection © 2001, Her Majesty Queen Elizabeth II; p 83 © photo RMN/Gérard Blot; pp 84, 85, 86, 87, 88 (t), 88(bl), 89, 90 & 91 Tatra, a s Koprivnice; p 88(br), photo: © Ed Lee/www.edleefoto.com; p 89, photo: Vaclav Jiru.

AD Architectural Design +
pp 94–7+ courtesy Battle McCarthy; p 98(t)+ courtesy Gigon + Guyer; pp 98(bl)+ & 98(br)+ © Heinrich Helfenstein, Zurich; p 99+ photos: © Heinrich Helfenstein, Zurich; p 100(t)+ photo: © Harald F Mueller, Germany; p 100(r)+ © Heinrich Helfenstein, Zurich); p 102 © Gigon + Guyer; p 104–8+ courtesy Toyo Ito & Associates, photos: Naoya Hatakeyama and drawings: © Toyo Ito & Associates, Architects; p 111+ © Teeple Architects.

Cover image: Christian Küsters
↪ CHK Design

Subscription Offices UK
John Wiley & Sons Ltd.
Journals Administration Department
1 Oldlands Way, Bognor Regis
West Sussex, PO22 9SA
T: +44 (0)1243 843272
F: +44 (0)1243 843232
E: cs-journals@wiley.co.uk

Subscription Offices USA and Canada
John Wiley & Sons Ltd.
Journals Administration Department
605 Third Avenue
New York, NY 10158
T: +1 212 850 6645
F: +1 212 850 6021
E: subinfo@wiley.com

Annual Subscription Rates 2001
Institutional Rate: UK £150
Personal Rate: UK £97
Student Rate: UK £70
Institutional Rate: US $225
Personal Rate: US $145
Student Rate: US $105

AD is published bi-monthly.
Prices are for six issues and include postage and handling charges.
Periodicals postage paid at Jamaica, NY 11431. Air freight and mailing in the USA by Publications Expediting Services Inc, 200 Meacham Avenue, Elmont, NY 11003

Single Issues UK: £19.99
Single Issues outside UK: US $32.50
Order two or more titles and postage is free. For orders of one title ad £2.00/US $5.00. To receive order by air please add £5.50/US $10.00

Postmaster
Send address changes to *AD* Publications Expediting Services, 200 Meacham Avenue, Elmont, NY 11003

Printed in Italy. All prices are subject to change without notice.
[ISSN: 0003-8504]

Looking Back in Envy
Guest-edited by Jan Kaplicky

Architectural Design +

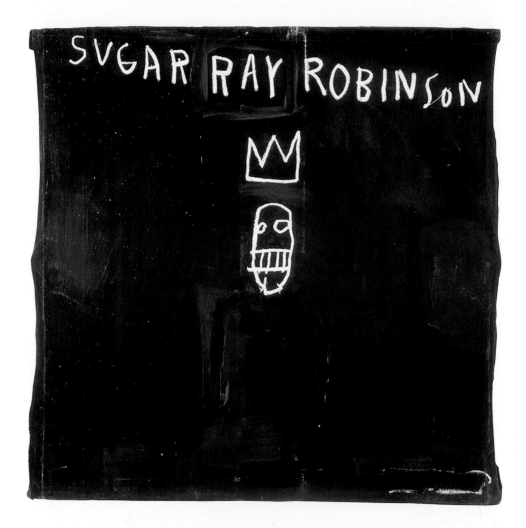

The starting point for this issue came in the form of a very straightforward observation from Jan Kaplicky of Future Systems. It had recently come to his attention that young architects have a very limited knowledge of 20th-century architecture and design - to the extent that they may not even be aware of iconic works such as the Eames House or the Maison de Verre in Paris. Kaplicky has already done much to arouse architectural creativity through his unique compilations of images, *For Inspiration Only* (Wiley-Academy, 1995) and *More For Inspiration Only* (Wiley-Academy, 1999); two volumes that singularly capture his preoccupations and passions for subjects as diverse as aeronautics, nature and modern architecture. In *Looking Back in Envy*, Kaplicky enforces the importance of the visual for architecture. In his introductory interview, for instance, he explains how during his youth in postwar Prague his parents' collection of back issues of *Life* provided him with a precious catalogue or resource of images. What particularly emerges afresh, though, here through Kaplicky's own description and that of his ten contributors is the importance of the experiential. In the case of both Jan Kaplicky and Tony Hunt, for instance, an early enthusiasm for modelmaking was to be formative, imbuing them with a unique understanding of how things work. Zaha Hadid also describes how over a number of years the experience of visiting cities, specifically New York, Brasília and Moscow, informed her own architecture.

On editing this issue, Jan was insistent that the ten contributors involved should have a broad remit. The only brief that they were given was to talk about objects, art works or architecture from the last century. As one might expect from a group of people who are used to stretching the boundaries and breaking the rules, on occasions this has been breached – with examples creeping in from earlier centuries. The result, however, is indisputably far-reaching and thought-provoking. For Klaus Bode, Director of consulting engineers BDSP Partnership, for instance, his choice of an Arctic dome designed by Ted Happold ignites a wider discussion on architecture and environmental engineering. Ron Arad's description of the work of the Colombo brothers focuses on an age-old conundrum that Joe and Gianni personified, as designers and artists: Is it preferable to be designing for a specified function or for art's sake? Brian Clarke and Anish Kapoor, the two artists who have contributed to this issue, have chosen to leave words behind and produce picture essays. Clarke's only verbal comment for his piece is that his choice relies very much on the moment – asked at any other time he would be bound to come up with a very different group of images – an important reminder of just how temporal any selection may be.

At a time when history, however recent, is generally regarded as little more than a source of nostalgia or the preservation of the heritage industry, *Looking Back in Envy* is intended to be a powerful reminder of the important part that retrospection has to play in innovation and looking forwards. For the ten dynamic forward-thinkers featured here, all found plenty to be envious of in the past in their predecessors' work.

Opposite
Jean Michel-Basquiat, *Untitled* (Sugar Ray Robinson), 1982 (The Brant Foundation, Greenwich, Connecticut). Acrylic and oilstick on canvas; 106.6x106.6x11.5cm/42x42x4.5 in. This painting by Michel-Basquiat is one of the images that Brian Clarke chose for his picture essay, 'Moving Target', pp 34–43.

Jan Kaplicky

Future Forward

Jan Kaplicky is the founding principal of Future Systems, the London-based practice whose work has become synonymous with innovative technologies and organic forms. The guest-editor of this issue of *Architectural Design*, he instigated the project through a firm belief in the importance of 'Looking Back' in order to look forwards. Here, he describes the formative influences of his youth in Czechoslovakia to Helen Castle, the editor of *D*, and explains how his youthful ambivalence about the past gave way to an unprejudiced interest in everything around him, new and old.

Most discussions about particular influences on artists and architects are restricted to the academic convention of relating one artist's work to another's. For Jan Kaplicky, this is more than an oversight. It is dishonest. For it fails to acknowledge the more familiar, yet formative influences on our lives, such as that of toys during childhood. As he says, 'The consequences of what you did when you were younger are frightening. They are so much stronger than when you are an adult.' Toys, as the first objects that you interact with, nurture creative skills but they also have material qualities that take on an almost iconic importance in the mind's eye. As a boy, Kaplicky's most prized possessions were a big blue bus and a caravan. The caravan had a very modern shape. It was white and had rubber wheels. The bus and caravan had a very profound influence on him. Their form and colour marked them out as American. Imported from the United State and Czech before the US went to war in 1941, they stood out from the German toys that were normally available.

For Kaplicky, the physical characteristics of toys were heightened by their acute shortage during and after the Second World War. Children born only a couple of years after him had to depend entirely on hand-me-downs as new toys went out of circulation. He was lucky enough to have a few toys of his own. They included a set of simple wooden cubes or building bricks invented by a Swiss educational expert. Unpainted, they were made from a variety of woods with very different qualities ranging from hard- to softwoods. One of his most coveted toys was a German Schuco car. He also had a metal aeroplane that could be assembled with screws. Like many others of his generation, he had a Meccano set, from which quite sophisticated constructions could be built. He had a German version, known as *Märklin*, which was black with brass wheels, and a Czech version, *Merkur*.

By his early teens, Kaplicky's main enthusiasm was for modelmaking. He assembled model aeroplanes from plans which he bought from a shop along with the required sheets of plywood and paper. These he stuck together with casein. Difficult to handle as a glue, casein is a milk product that comes in powdered form and has to be dissolved in water before it slowly goes hard.

There is a photograph of Kaplicky at the age of 14 sailing a magnificent model of a yacht. It is a miniature replica of the *Endeavour*, the British J-Class yacht that was completely built in steel for the 1934 America's Cup. Kaplicky constructed it entirely from drawings by a commercial artist that he found in a 1934 edition of the *Illustrated London News*. After completing the yacht he spent all his spare time – Saturday afternoons after morning school and Sundays – with a friend building an American warship or battleship from very bad photographs in magazines. This was followed by an aircraft carrier, which he never finished. However, the skills in drawing and relating photographs to constructions which Kaplicky acquired through his passion for modelmaking were to prove invaluable. As he explains, putting kits together also brings home the three-dimensional plasticity of parts – the very vivid realisation, for instance, that a fuselage is always different oval shapes.

When Kaplicky came to leave upper high school for a university course in architecture he submitted some of his drawings of aeroplanes, but they were considered irrelevant. Students were encouraged to submit work on a very narrow range of subjects – life drawings and perhaps the odd sketch of a rural church – as well as proving themselves proficient in mathematical formulae and Czech grammar. Once at university, the curriculum was equally limited. Students were encouraged to look backwards rather than forwards, dwelling on the heritage of the past. The turbulent events of the previous few years meant there was a certain comfort to be had from looking at castles rather than modern architecture. Little in the way of contemporary architecture had been built in Czechoslovakia since the war, and what did exist dated back to the 1930s. The history of modern architecture was certainly not taught. One of Kaplicky's only contacts with a broader architectural world was through a tutor who had worked in Le Corbusier's office. He, however, was more revealing in informal conversation than in his teaching.

The culture and stability that surrounded Kaplicky at home far outweighed anything he gleaned formally from his teachers. With his parents, he lived in an environment where every detail was thought through. Though they lived in an ordinary suburban house, his father had designed its modern interior, including its furniture, and garden. Kaplicky's father painted and sculpted and designed graphics and furniture – every medium was within his reach. He treated everything as art. It was his father who first brought Le Corbusier to Kaplicky's attention by giving him an original edition of

Opposite
The big blue toy bus Jan
Kaplicky owned as a child.

Above
These simple cubes or
building bricks were invented
by a Swiss educational
expert. Not only different
shapes, they were also made
of different woods.

Clockwise from right
Kaplicky at 14 sailing the
magnificent model he made of
the Endeavour, the all-steel
British yacht built for the 1934
America's Cup.

During Kaplicky's youth the
photographs in back issues
of *Life* magazine, which his
parents subscribed to until the
Communist takeover in 1948,
were an important visual
source.

Clockwork Schuco car.

Kaplicky owned both German
and Czech versions of
Meccano.

Opposite
The garden Kaplicky's father
designed for their family home
in Prague.

the architect's *Oeuvre complète*, his complete works, from 1910. It was, however, his mother who ignited Kaplicky's love for the natural and the organic which pervades Future Systems' architectural forms. She was a botanical illustrator who had a passion for detail and everything growing. Together his parents created a happy home which, during the war and the Communist era, was a refuge from the harsh realities of the outside world. Having lived through the First World War, his mother and father had their fun during the 1930s, but sadly neither survived Communism.

Kaplicky assimilated their interests and passions without even realising it. In his late teens and early 20s he was too busy rejecting the past and his roots to acknowledge what he had acquired from those around him.

Kaplicky assimilated their interests and passions without even realising it. In his late teens and early 20s he was too busy rejecting the past and his roots to acknowledge what he had acquired from those around him. In particular, his university's obsession with the historic nurtured in him an ambivalence about older buildings. As he says, 'I didn't realise the possibility of learning from the past for a long time. It made me like to look forward.' He had to seek out information on contemporary architecture and design where he could. As well as Le Corbusier's *Oeuvre complète* he had books on Ronchamp and Wright's houses. Reading Le Corbusier brought him to Mies van der Rohe and Oscar Niemeyer. Despite the retrospective enthusiasms of the teaching faculty, the university library was well stocked with foreign magazines that published contemporary projects. They held issues of *Architectural Design*, *Architectural Review*, *Architecture d'Aujord hui*, *Arts and Architecture*, *Bauen und Wohnen*, *Domus* and *Forum*.

Kaplicky remembers that a neighbour was still getting British *Vogue*. The gap between life in Prague and the world portrayed in the magazine was almost inconceivable. His own family's subscription to *Life* magazine had been stopped in 1948 within two weeks

Above
Thousands of bunkers were built in the Czech countryside in the five years preceding the German invasion. These two examples show how their concrete forms struck up a poetic, if unintentional, connection with the surrounding landscape.

Right
Future Systems, house in Wales, 1994 -8. This sophisticated underground home emerges from the ground in a way that is redolent of the prewar Czech bunkers.

of the Communist takeover. Nevertheless, its back issues with their expansive photographic coverage of all sorts of subjects from fashion to war remained an important visual source for him.

Certainly, the shortage of goods and products in the shops engendered in Kaplicky a cultural feeling for objects. In the postwar period there was a great deal of reuse of military hardware and he developed an interest in this. As he points out, except for the date stamped on the cutlery, there is little difference between a mess tin produced for the First World War and one made during the Second World War. At this time Kaplicky also became aware of fabrics through camping in ex-army-issue tents. Shortages meant that through necessity people learnt how things worked so that they could fix them themselves. Everyone had to mend their own motorbikes or cars. This imparted to Kaplicky the sort of understanding of physical realities – of metal and the importance of the tightness of a single screw – that is now rare among contemporary architects.

The war had created its own architecture. Before the German invasion, thousands of bunkers – 32,000 between 1935 and 1938 – were erected throughout Czechoslovakia. These were important for their use of concrete as a material and also for their connection to the surrounding countryside. When Kaplicky shows Future Systems' underground house in Wales at lectures, he juxtaposes it with an image of a Czech bunker – rendering explicit the influence these quickly-assembled dwellings had on his imagination.

Many of the buildings he first encountered through publications when he was a student have retained their relevance and resonance for him today. Perhaps the foremost of these is Le Corbusier's Ronchamp chapel. Its power for Kaplicky lies in its highly sculptural form and relative simplicity of materials. The walls, though rendered, are constructed out of a concrete frame with masonry infill – rubble taken from a former church on the site. Its mass and materiality is quite unique, very different from the plasticity of Kaplicky's other hero, Oscar Niemeyer. An unusual feature of Ronchamp, which Kaplicky was not aware of until he visited the chapel in 1986, is its sloping floor – it recedes ever so slightly. It is one of those qualities that is imperceptible from photographs and is only experienced on entering a building.

Kaplicky is keen to have the opportunity to see Brasìlia and Niemeyer's other works in Brazil. He

Right
Having first encountered the Ronchamp chapel through publications in Czechoslovakia, Kaplicky visited it for the first time in 1986.

Above
Oscar Niemeyer's Museum of
Contemporary Art in Nieterói.
Completed in 1997, it is as
surprising in form as
Niemeyer's earlier works in
Brasília.

Opposite
The roof terrace of Luis
Barragán's residence at Calle
Ramírez 14, Mexico City.
Barragán repeatedly
experimented with this small
rooftop space, redesigning,
repainting and
rephotographing it.

admires Niemeyer, above all else, for his
instinctive feeling for form. As he states:

His sketches are conceptually so strong
that they can be literally transferred from
the drawing board into reality. They lose
none of their power through the
transformation process. This is because
they do not depend on silly details. No one
ever talks about Niemeyer's door handles,
though he has designed some very fine
furniture. Many of his interiors are
remarkable in colour. It is the combination
of colour and shape that is so potent in his
work. This is apparent in his latest projects –
his new museum, and his projected library
which is again a complete surprise in terms
of form.

If Kaplicky is passionate about Niemeyer's
innate sense of colour and plasticity of form, he
is equally enthusiastic about the contribution of
two of Niemeyer's contemporaries: Roberto
Burle Marx and Luis Barragán. This is because

they championed the use of greenery in architecture –
an element that has remained largely undeveloped in
architects' work in recent years, with the notable
exception of Kathryn Gustafson, who is featured here
(see p 50). A painter and landscape architect, Burle
Marx was an essential force in the Brazilian modern
movement. He constructed 'paradise gardens' often
with plants dug straight out of the jungle. In contrast,
Barragán was an architect who became as famous for
his incorporation of landscape into his houses as he
was for his domestic designs. Watercourses, fountains
and lush vegetation were integral to the architecture of
his buildings. The houses can also be seen as a natural
and modern advance on traditional Mexican ones which
were built around courtyards.

Kaplicky similarly admires Pierre Chareau and
Bernard Bijvoet's Maison de Verre for the way it uses its
site, maximising on a very limited space. No one since
has done anything better in such confined urban
conditions. Built on the rue Saint-Guillaume, Paris,
between 1928 and 1931, the house is literally embedded
in a conventional urban block. It epitomises the classic

problem of the Anglo-American town house. Built for Chareau's son-in-law, it functioned as part gynaecological clinic and part private residence. When the woman who owned the top floor of the orginal building refused to move, the architects simply built around or, rather, beneath it; the top floor is propped up from below by a structural steel frame. This allows for a remarkable handling of space and a flexible plan. Though handmade, the various components have an industrial feel. Chareau, who had previously designed interiors, gates and staircases, collaborated with some of the finest metalworkers in Paris. The house gets its name from the expansive use of glass tiles on its elevation.

The last building Kaplicky describes is Une Petite Maison, a small house Le Corbusier built for his parents in 1923 on Lake Geneva. It is a building that Kaplicky has come to know and appreciate through the small book Le Corbusier wrote about it. Filled with drawings, it includes a sketch of his mother and a poetic passage describing how he first encountered the house's idyllic site. As well as being a beautiful object, this little book shows how essential observation was to Le Corbusier, whether through drawing, writing or architecture. As Kaplicky concludes, observation in any direction should be reflexive: 'Looking back is essential. Looking around is fundamental.' He warns that if we don't look, it is at our peril: 'Isolation starts, if you ignore things. Look at all those people who take no notice of changes taking place around them.' Not looking is not only limiting. 'It ultimately leads to involvement with things without any meaning.' ⚏

Ron Arad

Work that doesn't need to answer

When Edwin Heathcote went to talk to designer and architect Ron Arad, he was unable to pin him down to discussing any single object or series of objects. Instead, Arad described to him how he was inspired by the relationship of two brothers — Gianni and Joe Colombo — who epitomise his own desire to simultaneously create for art's sake and to work on projects with an explicit use or function.

If an artist makes an object that can be used, does it become art? Conversely, if a designer creates a work of art, is it design? The difficulty and, frankly, the irrelevance of the answers to these questions are embodied in the work of Ron Arad. Arad's career in design has been enriched by a consistent series of intersections between the sculptural, the playful and the useful. From designs like the *Concrete Stereo* (1984), which questioned the technical imagery of the electronics industry, or his exquisitely lyrical public sculpture, the *Windwand* in London's Canary Wharf (completed 2000) – a slender tower, or rather needle, which sways gently in the breeze like a reed – there has never been a clear delineation between art and design in Arad's work. Best known of all his designs is perhaps the Bookworm shelving (1994), which has become an icon of modern design as well as a staple of lifestyle shops and photo-shoots. For those few who don't know, the Bookworm is an ingenious piece of consumer installation-art that is both functional and sculptural. A single continuous band wanders up the wall, its surface interspersed with occasional hinged book ends which allow it to function as a shelf for books or anything else.

brother of Joe Colombo, the influential Milanese industrial designer. 'You can find parallels between the two Colombos.' Leafing casually through the pages Arad says, almost ruefully, 'I am a bit jealous of this world here.' Gianni Colombo remained an artist while his brother moved from his auspicious beginnings as an artist involved in the Concrete Art movement in the 1950s into architectural and industrial design, although the two brothers continued to work on some art projects together. Arad seems to have a little of each brother in him: a little art and little design.

'People think it has to be one or the other. In my case it is both; work for the studio or work for industry. It is work that doesn't need to answer. Gianni's work [Arad points to a photograph of a coiling and meandering sculpture that recalls his own Bookworm shelving] doesn't need to tell you if it's functional or decorative … He can just sculpt fittings.'

Arad's choice of the work of an artist rather than that of a designer is partly explained by his justification of his own individualistic and mannered designs. 'Modern furniture peaked in the 1950s. You can't do anything more advanced than a Jacobsen chair. I'm more interested in people who have passed the Jacobsen/Eames barrier and who introduce new things to the world.'

Presumably it is Arad's reluctance to differentiate between art and design that made him take a book on the work of an artist off the (Bookworm) shelf, as being the greatest influence on him, rather than a single work by a designer.

Presumably it is Arad's reluctance to differentiate between art and design that made him take a book on the work of an artist off the (Bookworm) shelf, as being the greatest influence on him, rather than a single work by a designer.
'The book which said "pick me" was this one on Gianni Colombo.' Gianni Colombo was the

Opposite left
Ron Arad, Bookworm shelving, 1994. The plastic, low-cost version of this bookshelf, produced by Kartell, is currently the Italian furniture manufacturer's best seller.

Opposite right
Ron Arad, *Concreto Stereo*, 1984. A playful sculpture questions the technical imagery of the electronics industry.

Right
Text-messaging sculpture planned for the corner of Berwick Street and Broadwick Street, Soho, London.

Opposite top left
Gianni Colombo, Reggiani Editore (Italy), 1999. This catalogue accompanied the retrospective exhibition 'Gianni Colombo: L'artista e il suo mondo' shown during the autumn of 1999 at the Sogetsu Art Museum in Tokyo.

Opposite top right
Gianni Colombo, *Spazio Curvio*, 1991.

Opposite bottom
Gianni Colombo holding his *Strutturazione Acentrica*, 1962.

Right
Gianni Colombo, *Strutturazione Fluida*, 1960–69.

Below
Gianni Colombo, *Spazio Curvio*, 1991.

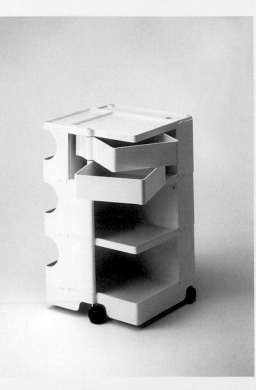

Top left
Joe Colombo, '"Boby" Trolley'
(52.5x40.5x43 cm), 1970.

Top right
Joe Colombo, 'Universale
Chair ' (height 72 cm), 1965.

Right
Joe Colombo 'Tavolo Lamp'.

ron
arad
associates

Above and right
Ron Arad's design for a 3,500-square-foot new technology floor for Selfridges in Oxford Street, London. A special feature of this cutting-edge department, which has a 24-hour media café, are the curved CD racks.

Arad certainly seems to be fulfilling his own criteria. He is currently working on a set of remarkable designs for the new technology floor of Selfridges in London's Oxford Street, which employs a system of CD racks, constructed from conveyor belts on curving and undulating ribbons, that allows a far greater ratio of shelf space to floor area. In a way, these elegant mechanisms are as much art and decoration as they are solutions to a practical problem. Although Arad bemoans the fact that 'kinetic art became unfashionable', what he is in effect doing is reinterpreting the movement and the delight in the crossover of the functional and the whimsical, of art and design which so intrigued the Colombo brothers. The new CD racks at Selfridges, like Arad's *Windwand* and like his new public art project at the junction of Berwick Street and Broadwick Street in London's Soho – a public text-messaging system using a pixellated scroll to display to the street messages keyed in by passers-by – are all types of interactive art. In the Bookworm shelving, Arad brought a kind of art on to the walls of modern homes which, once the similarities are pointed out to you (subtly, by Arad himself), was obviously inspired by the work of Gianni Colombo. Pointing to a typically undulating Colombo sculpture, a snaking form the coils of which seem to exude a springy energy and potential, Arad says, 'Look at this. It doesn't need to tell you if it is shelving or art.' The potential for function is inherent in the form. Arad's skill lies in seeing that potential and transforming art into the functional without losing the poetic. ∆

Edwin Heathcote is an architect, freelance journalist and writer.

Klaus Bode

Inspiration 'par hazard'

Here Jan Kaplicky's invitation to 'look back' prompts environmental engineer Klaus Bode to look beyond buildings as end products and to consider how essential the design process is for environmentally sensitive design. He explains how, somewhat ironically, his attention was first brought to engineering and the environment by Ted Happold's and Frei Otto's 1971 proposal for a futuristic Arctic City – a fantastical vision which, in reality, would have resulted in nothing less than environmental disaster.

Buildings are most frequently seen as end products in themselves. In 90 per cent of cases, only recently completed ones are documented. Feedback on occupational use is rare. Questions like how successful a building is and how well it performs technically or environmentally are rarely answered, or at least publicised, though buildings spend the rest of their lives being occupied. But the beginning or the 'idea' may be – and often is – not the same as, or even similar to, the end product. And why is that? Because the end product is fundamentally a consequence of the design process – the more successful the communication, the better the end product.

The 'key' parameters that affect the end product through the design process include: a common objective (client/design team) and clear understanding of one's objectives; effective communication; teamwork (genuinely seeking a common goal); inclusive rather than exclusive design methods; finance/costs; programme constraints; legislation (regulatory and planning constraints); and politics and time (affect changes in priority).

My enthusiasm for environmental engineering was born 'par hazard'. I was attracted by an article about designing an 'Arctic' city (Ted Happold/Frei Otto) – a large tensile structure that would cover a whole city whilst creating a totally 'artificial' environment in one of the world's harshest climates. It is ironic that such a proposal, which was potentially an energy-guzzler, resulted in a career spent pursuing interests in energy conservation. But as an 18-year-old, I found the quest of achieving the almost unachievable more attractive than the moral high ground. I enrolled in an environmental engineering course at the University of Bath that was coupled with two years of joint architecture and structural engineering. I am convinced that this early participation in, and understanding of, interdisciplinary activities are the foundations of my belief that 'improved' communication between the various parties constituting the design team is the road to future success. The outcome must be better buildings.

The terminologies used in describing low-energy design have been many and varied, with 'sustainability' virtually becoming a 'must' in architectural proposals or submissions, particularly competitions. But with what consequences? Although some ambitions towards energy efficiency may be genuine, others are more politically driven. Whatever the category, all too often truly environmentally-sensitive designs remain unrealised. And why is this the case?

'Low energy' or 'sustainable' design has become a fashion victim, lacking depth and credibility. It is intangible, only visible or identifiable over time (often over long periods of time), and as such is not immediately attractive to consumers and, particularly, investors. We are a consumer-driven society, seeking fast responses.

All too often, proposed design solutions appear to be 'restrictive', with clichéd analogies such as south-facing winter gardens, photovoltaic cells or solar collectors on pitched roofs, reduced areas of glazing, high levels of insulation, etc. In reality, a building that incorporates none of the above could be made to be more energy efficient. The issue is far more complex and far-reaching and, contrary to common belief, it is immeasurably flexible in terms of available options.

The philosophy on low-energy design can be summarised in three steps:
Step 1: Reduce the demand for energy
Step 2: Use renewable sources of energy to cover energy demand
Step 3: Use highly efficient technologies, with low-polluting sources of fuel, to cover outstanding energy demand (zero CO_2 buildings stop at Step 2).

Our focus should be on Step 1, including an understanding of the various energy needs – uses, demand profiles, functions, etc. Everything else is a consequence of this first step. It is by far the most important of the three as not only are buildings typically responsible for about 50 per cent of the world's energy demand, but they are generally the single most expensive investment commercial and public organisations will ever engage in – hence one must ask why such capital-intensive expenditure doesn't warrant longer payback periods (more than five to 10 years). The result is that modern examples of low-energy design are primarily domestic, with few public or commercial buildings that genuinely fit the definition.

Unlike the conventional approach to design, cutting-edge environmental design takes an all-encompassing approach, blurring the divide between architecture and engineering. Both parties should be allowed to transgress these so-called 'disciplinary boundaries' and venture proactively into each other's domain, always under the pretext of respecting the other's specific professional know-how. This blurring of the divide between the professions is necessary and should be actively encouraged (both through education and at work) to create not only successful buildings, but also to achieve (what I would call) a truly environmental or sustainable design solution. Vernacular architecture is riddled with exemplary buildings or structures. It dates from a time when technology was in its infancy and hence working with nature rather than against it was

Opposite bottom
Arctic City 58 Degrees North, Ted Happold with Frei Otto, Kenzo Tange and Ove Arup, 1971.

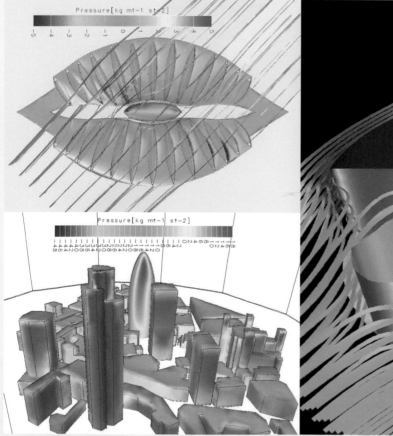

the only option. This approach also generated
an architectural 'identity', varied throughout the
world, that was synonymous with the climate
and with the materials at the builder's disposal.
Ironically, we have forgotten that art.

Today, we should theoretically be in a position
to better this approach through the relatively
quantum leaps in technological development and
the highly sophisticated analytical tools at our
disposal. We should challenge and expand the
basis of 'conventional' low-energy design by
reviewing and redefining design parameters,
re-evaluating the definition of 'comfort' by
recognising the importance of psychology as
well as physiology, allowing people choice and
'freedom' at work through occupant interaction
with space, and critically reappraising current
regulations and design standards. Increased
mobility and flexibility in the work place also
needs to be fed into the equation.

Such an approach requires the design team
and client (and where possible the ultimate
users of a building) to be 're-educated'. This may
at first seem ominous, and to some impossible,
but on closer analysis it could be easier than one
might at first expect. It must be in a language
that is understood by all. Quoting 'PPD'
percentages of five per cent or 15 per cent as
comfort indices is meaningless to most people –
communicating in terms of 'long' or 'short'

Borge Boeskov

Inflight Design

For its realisation, design often hinges on entrepreneurs and corporate leaders with vision. Betsy Case describes how in the mid-1990s Borge Boeskov, the president of Boeing Business Jets, identified a new market for luxury customised jets. Boeskov and the designers of the jets' interiors have taken their inspiration from the first half of the 20th century – a golden age of air travel with the Model 80, the Boeing Clipper and the Stratocruiser.

`The Boeing Business Jet is a product of its time. As the number of people travelling by air increases year by year, the jet-setting elite class of passengers swells accordingly. The decision by the Boeing Company and General Electric to team up in 1996 to produce the Boeing Business Jet (BBJ) was driven by global executives' and VIPs' demands for executive jets with greater space, comfort and utility. A modified Boeing 737, the Business Jet provides owners with an unprecedented amount of space which can be transformed into formal dining rooms, comfortable executive suites and business conference areas.

Borge Boeskov, however, explains that the BBJ was a long way from being the first executive aeroplane produced by Boeing. The company understood the needs of VIP travellers as far back as 1929 when the Boeing Model 80, designed especially for passenger comfort and convenience, made its first flight. Boeskov says William Boeing was a visionary who 'understood what airplane travel could do for him and his business. A corporate leader or VIP of today can easily understand and relate to the way Bill Boeing was thinking in the early 30s.'

The Model 80 was elegantly appointed with leather seats, wicker furniture and gleaming brass reading lamps. It – much like the Boeing Business Jet – had enough room for passengers to walk freely around the cabin, dine in style and sleep comfortably. The aeroplane caught the eye of Standard Oil of California, who had it modified with special features and then used it to transport executives in the height of luxury in the early 1930s. It was, in fact, the first real executive aeroplane.

Early interior design elements for the Model 80 and its successors, the Boeing Clipper and Stratocruiser, were an attempt to bring the warmth of the home to air travel.

Opposite
The Model 226, a version of the Boeing Model 80A, was significantly modified with special features in 1930 to provide comfortable transport for the executives employed by Standard Oil of California. In essence, this was the first real executive aeroplane.

Right
Much like the Boeing Business Jet, Standard Oil's executive aeroplane offered comfortable seating and room to move around the cabin, allowing passengers to work or relax en route to their business destination.

Above
The Model 80A was like a ship or a railway coach with all the latest interior fashions of the time. The aeroplane was decorated with wicker furniture that served two purposes according to Boeskov: 'It was elegant and it was lightweight.'

Right
Beige mohair wallcoverings and upholstery, wood trim and brass reading lights with fabric shades provided all the comforts of home for passengers travelling in the Model 80A. The completely restored Model 80A shown here is on display at the Museum of Flight in Seattle, Washington.

Early interior design elements for the Model 80 and its successors, the Boeing Clipper and Stratocruiser, were an attempt to bring the warmth of the home to air travel, according to Don Thompson of Donald Thompson Industrial Design of New York City. Thompson is a member of the oPen Group, which consists of a few hand-picked designers who are in the process of creating numerous BBJ interiors. 'There was a different feeling to airplane interiors back then,' says Thompson. 'Transportation was much more romanticised. The travel experience was more important than the actual journey.'

Craig Leavitt of Leavitt and Weaver in Los Angeles, also a member of the oPen Group, says many of the old ideas have been lost in the shuffle. 'We want to incorporate those ideals in today's BBJ designs,' he says. 'There is an interest in seeing past interior quality come back in its simplicity. Everything is very functional but there are beautiful fabrics and textures.' He cites the Boeing Clipper, introduced in June of 1938, as an example to emulate. Embroidered silk adorned the dining-room walls of the one that transported US president Franklin Roosevelt to Casablanca to meet Winston Churchill in 1943.

Boeskov says Roosevelt's requirements were, in fact, very similar to those of today's executives. The US

Above
Introduced in 1938, the 314 Clipper – a flying boat named after ocean-going sailing ships – was developed by Boeing in response to a request by Pan American Airlines for an aeroplane that could comfortably transport passengers across the ocean.

Right
The elegant dining salon in the 314 Clipper was able to compete with some of the world's finest restaurants. Four-star hotels provided airborne gourmet meals served in a luxurious setting enhanced by fresh flowers, sparkling crystal and crisp white linen.

Above
In 1943 President Franklin D Roosevelt celebrated his birthday in a Pan American Airlines Clipper that had been pressed into military service. The silk wallcovering in the dining room was embroidered with a map of the world – a fitting setting for a global leader. Roosevelt, flanked by his military adviser, was returning home from the Casablanca Conference.

Right
Between meals the Clipper's dining salon was transformed into a comfortable lounge where passengers could while away the time it took to cross the ocean in the late 1930s and early 1940s. This versatility is also evident in today's Boeing Business Jet.

Far right
In 1945, Pan American Airways placed an order for 20 Stratocruisers. Boeing and Pan Am hailed the transaction as 'opening a new era for global mass transportation of passengers ... in unprecedented comfort and the highest standard of reliability.'

Right
'The BBJ benefits from the heritage of the Stratocruiser that allowed passengers to not only travel in comfort and luxury, but to be ready for business – or whatever – upon arrival,' says Boeing Business Jets' president Borge Boeskov.

Below left
The Stratocruiser set new standards in sumptuous air travel with gold-appointed dressing rooms, a state-of-the-art galley and a circular staircase that led to a lower-deck cocktail lounge with seating for 40 passengers.

Below right
The forerunner of the Stratocruiser, the Stratoliner, was introduced in 1938. Multimillionaire Howard Hughes turned his own personal Stratoliner into a flying penthouse complete with a master bedroom, two bathrooms, galley, bar and palatial living room.

Right
A dining room resplendent with crystal and fresh flowers is reminiscent of the Stratocruiser and Clipper. Like the Clipper, this BBJ dining area is convertible – in this case to a no-nonsense conference room with a flat-screen projector for viewing business presentations.

Far right and below
The two BBJ lounge areas shown here display the versatility of the BBJ. One is designed like a comfortable club car, the other is created for team seating. Craig Leavitt of Leavitt and Weaver says, 'With materials, colours and textures, the interior can be changed to look totally different.'

president needed to have his team with him and it was imperative that he save time – travelling by sea would have taken him the better part of 20 days. Instead the journey took just a few days, he was able to travel in comfort, and arrived relaxed and ready to meet the challenges of his office.

The Boeing Stratocruiser is also part of the BBJ's legacy, says Boeskov. 'From the Stratocruiser, the BBJ inherited the idea of travelling not only in comfort and luxury, but of being ready for business – or whatever – when you got off the airplane.' The Stratocruiser was the epitome of airline luxury when it was introduced in 1947. Passengers were pampered with gold-appointed dressing rooms and a formal dining salon complete with crisp white linens and fresh flowers. A graceful spiral staircase led from the main cabin to a lower-deck cocktail lounge.

The interiors of recently completed BBJs have a great deal in common with the Boeing aeroplanes of the past, says Thompson. 'A majority display a lot of similarity with the Clipper and Model 80, for example, in terms of luxury and comfort.' Boeskov says some BBJ interiors are 'truly astounding'. He describes ones with fluted Grecian columns, hand-stitched leather seats and walls of gleaming hand-crafted inlaid wood.

In the vein of creating early Boeing aeroplane interiors that made passengers feel at home, the oPen Group team has designed a Sky Home concept for a new BBJ. Thompson describes it as both a home and an office, taking a lot of its design thinking from an individual residence. 'There are comfortable, cosy public spaces like you'd find in a library or English men's club.'

There's never been anything quite like the Sky Home concept, according to Leavitt, who says this BBJ can be both a home and an office. 'We had to cross both lines – the warm, relaxing home atmosphere and the productive business atmosphere – to meet the criteria of the owner.'

Meeting the criteria of BBJ owners can be a challenge says Thompson. 'You have a wide audience and marketplace with a variety of demands. You have to match the personality of the individual or the corporation with the interior design. You have to look at their lifestyles and how they want to be perceived.' The ultimate goal, according to Leavitt, is to give people what they want in a custom-made VIP aeroplane.

Harking back to the elegant touches of the past, such as the brass wall-sconces of the Model 80, the shimmering silk walls of the Clipper and the Stratocruiser's imaginative use of space, it seems that the design of aeroplane interiors has come almost full circle. Says Thompson: 'With the BBJ, the experience of travelling is fulfilling once again.' ⌂

Clockwise from top

Taking a page from the Stratocruiser design, the BBJ has enough space for full-sized amenities including a well-appointed bathroom with a high-tech recirculating shower available as a customer option.

The master suite in the BBJ easily accommodates a plush queen-sized bed where executives can retire for a moment of quiet reflection or a good night's sleep.

Some Boeing Business Jets are all business, designed with first-class team seating and a conference room that connects directly to the home office and the world from an on-board communications centre.

Brian Clarke

Moving Target

Architectural artist Brian Clarke is internationally renowned for his designs for stained-glass windows. His architectural projects, which also include the use of mosaic and tapestry, and his paintings can be found throughout the world. Clarke holds a unique position at the interface of art and architecture. As Lord Foster explains, he is 'one of those few artists who understands the spatial world of architecture – the core issues of space and light.' For his contribution to 'Looking Back', Clarke opted for a picture essay: a purely visual comment on his preoccupations which, rather than being definitive, are forever shifting and developing.

Right
Albert Speer, 'Cathedral of Light' for the 1934 Party Congress in Nuremburg. (Bayerischer Staatsbibliothek, Munich.)

Opposite
Jeff Koons, *Puppy*, 1992, (The Brant Foundation, Greenwich, Connecticut, courtesy Anthony d'Offay Gallery). Oil and inks on canvas; 305x427cm/ 120x168in.

'Dependent upon changing interests and moods, one's choice of the pivotal art events of the century also changes. The choices represented here reflect the mood of a single day, the day I chose them. The day after they might easily have been entirely different.'
—Brian Clarke

Opposite top
Pablo Picasso, *The Studio*, 1928
(Museum of Modern Art, New
York). Oil on canvas; 149.5x195
cm (59x77 in).

Opposite bottom
Henri Matisse, altar in the
Chapelle du Rosaire, Vence,
France, 1947–51.

Above
Jackson Pollock, *Blue poles*,
1952 (National Gallery of
Australia, Canberra. Enamel
and aluminium paint with glass
on canvas; 212.09x488.95cm/
83.5x92.5in.

Right
Charles Rennie Mackintosh,
guest bedroom, 78 Derngate,
Northampton, 1916–17
(Hunterian Art Gallery,
University of Glasgow,
Mackintosh Collection).

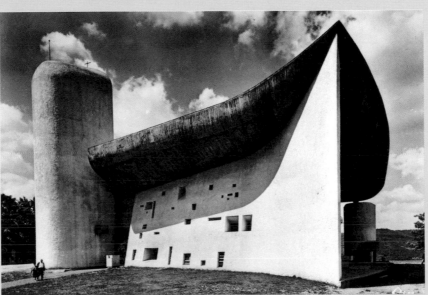

Opposite
Francis Bacon, *Study after Velasquez*, 1950 (The Estate of Francis Bacon, courtesy Tony Shafrazi Gallery, New York). Oil on canvas; 198 x137.2 cm/ 78x54in.

Above
Norman Foster, Willis Faber and Dumas, Ipswich, 1974.

Right
Le Corbusier, Chapel Ronchamp, Belfort, France, 1955–59.

40

Opposite
Gilbert and George, *Coming*,
1983 (private collection).
16-panel photo piece;
241x201cm/95x79in.

Right
David Bailey, 'The Kray Twins',
1965 (private collection).
Black-and-white photographic
print.

Bottom
Ralph Gibson, 'Quadrants',
1975 (private collection).
Black-and-white photographic
print.

Above
Richard Hamilton, *Swingeing London*, 1968/9 (private collection). Oil on canvas; 67.3x85cm/26.5x33.5in.

Right
Jean Michel-Basquiat, *Untitled* (Sugar Ray Robinson), 1982 (The Brant Foundation, Greenwich, Connecticut). Acrylic and oilstick on canvas; 106.6x106.6x11.5cm/ 42x42x4.5in.

Opposite
Andy Warhol, *Electric Chair*, 1964 (private collection, courtesy Tony Shafrazi Gallery, New York). Silkscreen ink on synthetic polymer paint on canvas; 55.8x121.9cm/ 22x48in).

Peter Cook

Clorindo Testa's Bank of London and South America, Buenos Aires

Peter Cook, co-founder of Archigram and current Bartlett Professor and Chairman of Architecture at University College London, describes the revelation he experienced during the early 1960s when he came into contact with photographs of Clorindo Testa's Bank of London and South America in Buenos Aires. The building diverted him from the more usual enthusiasms of architectural students of the time – for Oscar Niemeyer and Scandinavian modernism – and ignited in him what was to become a lifetime's passion for layered facades, curved holes and richly formatted concrete.

In the late 1950s, as befitted an unashamed provincial just come up to London, I eagerly scoured the architectural magazines. Until recently I had maintained my enthusiasm for the 'new', and had tiptoed past British 'reasonableness' sustained by glimpses of (mostly) black-and-white photographs of the audacious (contraptions to amplify the Smithsons' statements), the exotic (Niemeyer or Villanueva from the south) and the haunting (Asplund from the north or Scharoun from the east).

Then suddenly there was this funny, lovely thing full of holes – TV-shaped holes it would seem. It was big, it was built and it was in an exotic-sounding country far from home. Without realising it, I was already rolling towards the love affair with layers and screens that would come to characterise my own work. I was devouring every piece of evidence of forms that could dig into creamy, gooey, cave-ish aspects of concrete.

Of course, I had been properly brought up as a child of poured concrete: to appreciate the pioneering work of Perret, to hero-worship Le Corbusier from afar and to note with due seriousness the inexorable link between the rational and the constructible in European modernism. But I was gripped by something more in Clorindo Testa's bank: the freshness of its facade, the deepness of its holes. The hint of layers behind and within.

It suffered the same fate as Ludwig Leo's work in Berlin: treated as somehow supra-architectural and of an iconography too difficult to categorise.

Over time the memory dimmed a little. In the intervening 20 years the bank was rarely published and almost never referred to in polite European architectural circles. It suffered the same fate as

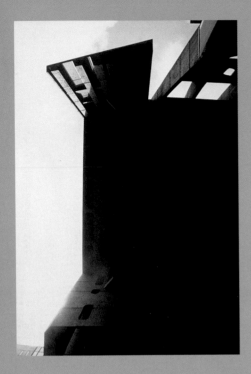

Ludwig Leo's work in Berlin: treated as somehow supra-architectural and of an iconography too difficult to categorise. More puzzling, in retrospect, was the fact that it seemed never to be mentioned by my Japanese friends, who had developed a healthy taste for the curved hole and richly formatted concrete.

On a two-day buzz down from São Paulo I finally saw the thing. So much richer, so much more layered, so much cleverer than in the grainy photographs. And immaculately tailored. Its urbanity matched only by its author's.

Testa is a genial and assured human being. The naughtiness and continued vigour of his drawings, his sculptures and his buildings, and his role as reference and sage for the Buenos Aires scenery, are belied by his appearance. He could be a successful lawyer or banker, in a camelhair coat and inevitably pulling on a cigarette. On site, however, there is no smooth talk. He took us around to all key points from which one could appreciate the tightness of four

street corners, so that one could suddenly 'twig' the significance of the strange drooping concrete eyelid: trapping the shadow of the banking hall and turning the three corners of the other buildings into definitions of an even more exotic 'room' than the hall itself.

A virtuoso stroke that is only hinted at by photographs.

Without disappearing from my mind, the powerful holes in the outer skin stepped back into their legitimate role as but one of a series of devices that deal with light, territory and layering in a way that is rarely seen outside one or two of the subtlest Gothic ambulatories. Furthermore, the tailoring of the concrete skirts inwards towards pavement level, and the smaller scale tailoring of staircases and balconies within, is both more relaxed and more original than devices in the concrete banks by his Japanese contemporaries.

Like the man, the whole thing is knowing, steady and gently heroic.

Opposite left
Under the eyelid.

Opposite right
The opposite side of the street as a wall of the 'room' of the bank.

Above
The four corners of the street – about to be captured by an eyelid.

On my return to Europe I found myself endlessly crowing about the building – as with Leo's work using any sleight of hand to incorporate it into almost any lecture topic. The young, the brainwashed and the far away had to be told, for here was something that all of Eisenman's swotting or Moneo's cleverness would never be able to achieve: a form of architectural knowingness that uses space and surface with such deftness. So what if it was in the 'wrong place at the wrong time' for 1980s and 1990s audiences? For me it is like a directive – to remember to enclose, to layer and to shield, and to let the shapes come as they must.

Two return visits and discussions with many friends (speakers at Glusberg's Buenos Aires biennales) have served to enlarge the Testa fan club and (I suspect) to give Prix or Mayne or Hecker (not one of them a slouch when turning a corner) a bit to think about. Accumulating one's own *experienced* references one thinks about about Gaudí's corners, about Isozaki's Oita law courts, about Miralles' cemetery and, of course,

about late Corb. But Testa's bank is more Gothic than any of these. Inexplicably both brooding and jolly: like a Wagner finale.

Clorindo came over to the Bartlett a few months ago, typically relaxed and bursting with observation and energy. Of course, I was far too shy to reveal how important his bank has been to me, both at the level of formal reference and of cultural pointer.

As a formal reference it suggests that a bold manoeuvre towards the site needs sometimes to be made; and that if this means inventing an odd – even ungainly – device, so be it. If this means treating territory in an audacious way: so be it, again. It also suggests that one should not be afraid of bold mannerisms of surface: surely they will survive the temporary label of 'style'.

As a cultural pointer it reinforces one's frustrated cry that, however many photographs, videos, texts, descriptions or even models there are, some architecture has to be seen to be believed.

Save up for the ticket, enjoy a good steak and wander into the corners of this knockout building. ◬

Kathryn Gustafson

The Recurrent Ring

The landscape architect Kathryn Gustafson describes how *The Magic Ring*, a red travertine sculpture by Isamu Noguchi, has 'the most direct correlation' with her work. Nicola Kearton talked to Gustafson about the analogies between the *Ring* and her landscape designs, and shows here how it reverberates in Gustafson's ideas about the relationship between art and nature.

about the relationship of man and the environment had a profound effect on her. Born in America, she trained at the École Nationale Supérieure du Paysage, Versailles, and then settled in France where she became a leader in the relatively new field of French corporate landscape design. To date, many of her best-known pieces including Shell headquarters at Rueil-Malmaison, Rights of Man Square in Évry and L'Oréal headquarters in Aulnay-sous-Bois, are in France. Since 1997 she has spent half her time in the United States and in 2000 opened a partner practice based in Seattle. Her US projects include the terrace for the American Museum of Natural History in New York and the intriguing skeletal structure of the pedestrian bridge at South Coast Plaza, Costa Mesa, California. Incidentally, this is also the site of one of Noguchi's most acclaimed garden designs, 'California Scenario', completed in 1984.

Not restricting herself purely to landscapes, Gustafson has been quoted as saying that she will design 'anything with a sky'[2], and one of her most notable forms has been the high-tension pylons for Electricité de France designed with Ian Ritchie and RFR Engineers for use in sensitive areas of natural beauty. Inspired by the long neck and head of a heron reaching into the sky, these structures bring an extraordinary grace and serenity to the function of transmitting electricity. She has also opened an office in London in 1997 with architect Neil Porter where a significant body of projects includes an 'indoor' landscape, the 'sky' being formed by the enormous domed glasshouse built by Foster and Partners for the National Botanic Garden of Wales.

Her highly intuitive method of design, which stems from an intense involvement with site and context and a natural sense of awe and respect for the natural world, the simplicity of her materials, and her sense of texture and colour all resonate with Noguchi's work. Noguchi was said to have always 'talked to his stone, the raw material from which his creations would emerge, before he started to work.'[3] Gustafson feels that it is impossible to do nature – that you have to listen to it

Looking at the sculptured ripples of earth around the Morbras storm reservoir, or the sensuous drapes of grass-covered bank at the Shell headquarters, Rueil-Malmaison, it is not hard to see why landscape designer Kathryn Gustafson chose Noguchi's Magic Ring (1970) as the object which had inspired her most. Although the nature of her work is of course different, developed from complex briefs and commissioned by large international organisations, it is marked by a unique creative vision that echoes some of the concerns expressed by Noguchi during his long creative life.

The Japanese-American sculptor Isamu Noguchi (1904–88) was studio assistant to Constantin Brancusi in Paris and travelled extensively between Asia, America and Europe. He expanded his concept of sculpture as the creation of lived space[1] into an extraordinary variety of fields which combined seminal modernist stage sets for the choreographer Martha Graham, furniture, product design and a passion for landscape. Noguchi designed many public and corporate gardens, plazas, memorials and playgrounds, and his influence on the emerging landscape designers of the 1960s and 1970s was immeasurable.

Similarly peripatetic, Kathryn Gustafson started as a fashion designer in New York. In the 1970s she moved into landscape design where her prolific output is marked by a strong sculptural sensibility. It was an era also marked by the emergence of the American Land Artists, whose epic sense of scale and radical ideas

and draw things from it and 'have it fit like a glove'.[4]

Noguchi felt strongly that the roots of his sculpture lay in the earth itself: like many of his generation he was also very drawn by prehistory and its remains. Gustafson expresses similar sentiments, finding, 'ancient cultures and the way that they had their own communication with the earth outside of agriculture important'. She suggests that her work is very much related to the ground – to its history but also to its present. She herself has drawn considerable inspiration from the arid and elemental landscape of her place of birth, Yakima, a small town in the centre of Washington State. Yakima is on a high plateau desert, surrounded by rugged mountains and huge skies, and, as she says, the earth there 'is naked'. It is also a landscape that is highly worked over with irrigation channels – there is less than 10 inches of rainfall a year – and dams built by the US Army Corps of Engineers,[5] so it is

a landscape that is both elemental and artificial.

As Gustafson says, *The Magic Ring* is the piece that perhaps has the most direct correlation with her own work, containing some of the elements that best summarise her own creative philosophy. As she did not have an image of the sculpture when we met, she reached for a pen and drew a sweeping circular shape on her pad. Instead of forming a ring, the two ends do not meet but instead one reaches inwards as if repelled by the other, suggesting a spiral. 'It must be made of many stones, it starts out thicker and gets thin, it's not a perfect shape and it's not a perfect spiral. With Noguchi's work, sometimes, there's this limit between nature and man. His materials are very natural, stone, water – you know that man has made it but it talks about things that are natural.'

For Gustafson it is this imperfection that gives the sculpture its tension – as she says, 'Nature is more perfect than that'. The piece has undergone a transformation and it inhabits a zone somewhere between the man-made and the natural. The

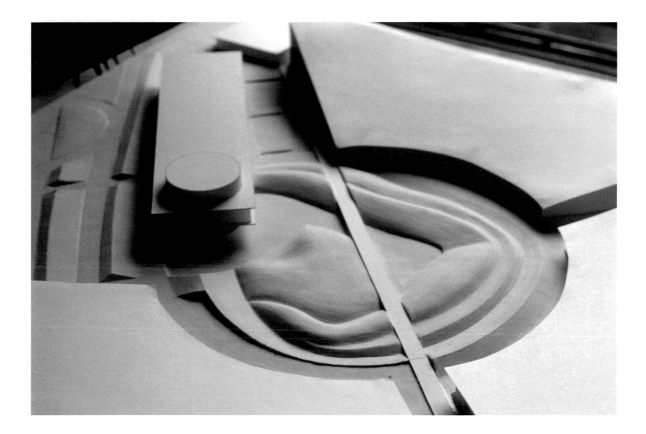

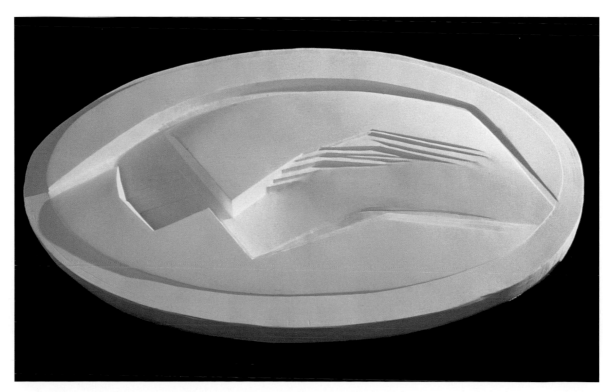

Top
Model for L'Oréal, Aulnay-sous-Bois (completed 1992). Spiralling canals and mounds of earth swirl towards the centre of the circle. 'I do not know why I do those movements but I just know they feel right. I am a very intuitive designer. There is intellectualism but it's not something which comes with words, it's just something which comes from spending hours in a place, something which fits, feels right.'

Bottom
Gustafson Porter, model for the National Botanic Garden of Wales (completed 1999). The 'indoor' landscape supports a collection of endangered plant species from the Mediterranean; the 'sky' is formed by the enormous domed glasshouse built by Foster and Partners. A dramatic axis is formed by a jagged ravine cutting across the site which has been excavated downwards to increase the feeling of space.

impossibility of replicating nature appears to be one of the central tenets of Gustafson's work: 'Landscape architecture has very little to do with nature, it is a design ... it can never replace nature, but it echoes and creates an environment that is in contact with the natural elements.' The land and what is hidden within it has been absorbed and from this there comes a strong conceptual statement that is also very contemporary.

Organic, circular forms obviously come very naturally to Gustafson. One only need look at the exquisitely sculptural models that form the basis for her projects – Morbras, L'Oréal, the landscape for the National Botanic Garden of Wales – to find intense circular shapes that seem to bore downwards into the body of the earth. As she says, 'I do not know why I do those movements but I just know they feel right. I am a very intuitive designer. There is intellectualism, but it's not something which comes with words, it's just something which comes from spending hours in a place, something which fits, feels right.'

Gustafson first saw *The Magic Ring* at the *40 Years of Sculpture* exhibition at the Guggenheim in New York in 1985. Looking at it from above, she was struck not only by its colour – it is a

warm red – but by the way it related architecturally to the spiralling interior of the museum, placed as it was down at entrance level. Its scale also allowed the viewer to walk in it and around it, as well as look down on it, providing a constantly changing visual dynamic. Looking upwards, the ceiling of the Guggenheim became a 'sky' and, with the viewer animating the space, *The Magic Ring* took on some of the properties of a landscape piece. As Gustfason says, 'It talks about things which a landscape uses', echoing the way a landscape design has to work with the existing architecture. This is seen to striking effect in the Rights of Man Square, Évry, where a raised water channel in dark green granite links the entrances of the Mario Botta cathedral with the other public buildings around the square, creating a sense of cohesion. This aproach extends also to her work within corporations such as L'Oréal where her design links disparate sections of the organisation, creating avenues for communication.

Movement and interaction with people – Noguchi's concept of 'lived space' – are vital to Kathryn Gustafson. 'The body is very important in what we do and how it moves through space and how it feels in space, whether it feels comfortable or safe.' She uses the word 'happy' to summarise how one should feel in a Gustafson landscape. This is certainly borne out in the way her projects have matured and are used today. On a hot summer's day, protected from the traffic, lunchers

Above
The Ross Terrace, American Museum of Natural History, New York (completed 2000). Anderson & Ray Landscape Architects; Polshek and Partners, Planetarium Architects. Linking the historic museum building and the new modern planetarium with its floating moon-like sphere both physically and metaphorically, the concept was inspired by an illustration of the multiple, conical shadows cast by the moon during an eclipse. The design hints at the importance of recognising the historical basis of knowledge when new frontiers in science are pursued.

Right
EDF pylons, France (completed 1998). A collaboration with Ian Ritchie and RFR Engineers, these pylons for the Electricité de France were designed for use in sensitive areas of natural beauty. Inspired by the long neck and head of a heron reaching into the sky, these structures bring an extraordinary grace and serenity to the function of transmitting electricity.

crowd the Rights of Man Square in Évry, performances are staged and children and dogs play in the jets of water that squirt unexpectedly as sensors are triggered. Gustafson's experience of living in France with its successful tradition of well-used public parks with their intense theatricality has given her a strong feeling about the importance of design and of clearly delineated areas where the user knows exactly what each space is for. 'Happy' includes not only the body but the mind, which should be challenged: 'A challenge is often a happiness to certain people'.

Her projects are replete with associations that viewers who choose to can make with what existed before: she sees the fields of water jets at Évry as echoing the long wavy grasses of the pastures that were there before the town was developed. Aspects of her designs refer, perhaps abstractly, to the history of an organisation or help to reinforce its image. Hence the Ross Terrace at the American Museum of Natural History in New York links the historic museum building with the new planetarium, suggesting the evolving nature of scientific investigation and the importance of recognising the historical basis of knowledge.

Happiness is something that is common to all Gustafson's projects, whether they are for large corporate clients, where the landscape creates a human scale for individuals to work in, relieving the tedium involved in repetitious tasks – or the many land reclamation schemes she has been involved in where her expertise has been used in 'mending' a damaged environment such as the disused and polluted industrial Westergasfabriek site in Amsterdam, one of her latest projects, which is set to become a public park. ⌂

For many years the Editor of *Art & Design*, Nicola Kearton is now a freelance editor and writer.

Notes
1. Bruce Altshuler, 'Isamu Noguchi: Art Into Life'; reproduced on the Noguchi web site. For other useful information about Noguchi see www.noguchi.org/research.html.
2. Chris Young, 'Expanding Horizons', interview in *Landscape Design*, 277 (February 1999), pp 42–43.
3. Obituary of Isamu Noguchi, *The Japan Architect*, vol 64, no 4 (April 1989), p 5.
4. This and other quotations from an interview with the author in London, 15 March 2001.
5. Leah Levy, *Kathryn Gustafson: Sculpting the Land*, Spacemaker Press (Washington, DC), 1998.
6. Isamu Noguchi, *The Isamu Noguchi Garden Museum*, Abrams (New York, London), 1987, p 66.

Right and opposite
Model for the pedestrian bridge at South Coast Plaza, Costa Mesa, California (completed 2000). Bridge collaboration: James Poulson with Ellerbe Becket Architects; Plaza: Anderson & Ray Landscape Architects. This ethereal structure with its swooping form demonstrates Gustafson's ability to build things other than landscapes. As she says, 'I design anything with a sky'.

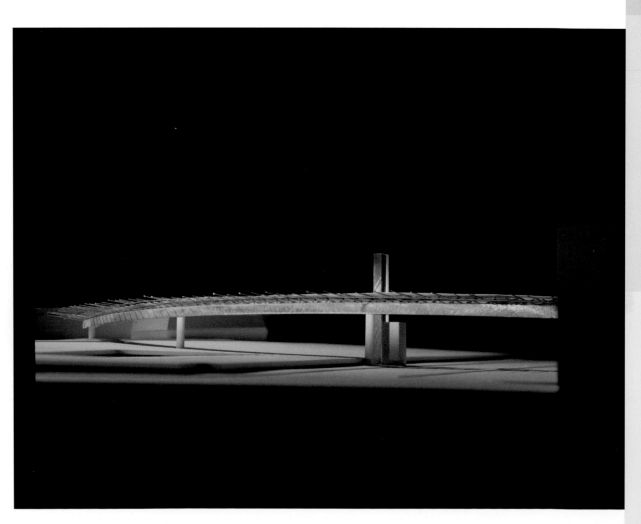

A Conversation with Zaha Hadid

A Tale of Three Cities

New York

Brasìlia

Moscow

The architecture of Zaha Hadid is complex and multilayered, as rendered by her beautiful paintings and computer-generated images. During an interview with Iain Borden, Hadid describes to him how she has realised the 'broader possibilities of urban architecture' through trips to three specific cities – New York, Brasìlia and Moscow.

Talking to Zaha Hadid and trying to identity a particular object upon which she might look back in envy, two things become immediately apparent. (1) There is no such singular object to be identified. (2) Any such objects, such as they are identifiable, are of uncertain quality and indirect connection with her own work. This much is, of course, to be expected: Hadid's work is in itself highly complex and layered, and so is not about to be unlocked by quick reference to an old item of furniture, famous art piece, ingenious building, thingamabob or whatchamacallit. Instead, Hadid typically locates her architectural conditioning in a much wider sphere: 'One of the greatest discoveries of the last 20 or so years is that one is not only influenced by architecture, but one is influenced by so many different things ... film, dance, fashion ... The idea of context no longer means the physical space surrounding buildings, and now can mean a variety of things which are as critical as a site boundary.'

So where does one look for this kind of complexity? What kind of object is it that offers such a range of cultures, spaces and experiences? Where else, but the city. And in a conversation which revolves around numerous cities – Beirut, Rio, Berlin, Paris, Tokyo, Chicago, LA, Havana, Chandigarh, São Paulo, London and Shanghai among others – three in particular stand out, to which Hadid returns again and again.

Opposite
Zaha Hadid, *New York, Manhattan: a new calligraphy of plan*, 1986.

Right
Zaha Hadid, *Painting of slabs, the Peak Club, Hong Kong*, 1982-83.

Top
Zaha Hadid, painting of 42nd
Street, New York, 1995.

Middle
Zaha Hadid, tram station,
Strasbourg.

Bottom
Zaha Hadid, computer image
of the Contemporary Art
Centre, Rome, 2001.

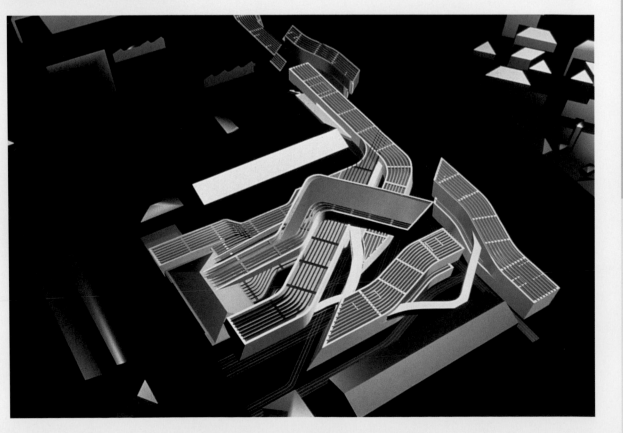

New York

Hadid went to New York during her fourth year of architectural study and, despite having travelled extensively as a child, it is clear that this education-oriented journey had a profound impact on her architectural development. In part, this was the immediate experience of particular buildings: the UN Headquarters is one Hadid notes. But beyond the specificity of single works Hadid also saw what they represented in terms of the possibility of urban architecture:

> What was so interesting about trips to places like New York was that you discovered things that you had thought about, and these trips showed that these ideas could indeed be done. When you saw a building like the Iron Flat, Rockefeller Center or Chrysler Building, these were evidence of real achievements of interior urban life and the possibilities of achieving great things through architecture.

Hadid's envy for New York is not then envy of particular buildings, but of a certain possibility, a sense of what might be the potential of architecture, in the broadest possible sense of 'potential', to impact upon the urban.

Her interest in New York is also the desire for a particular urban condition of strangeness and uncertainty. 'New York had an edge, surprises, erraticness. It was disturbing, dense and tense. One had to zigzag across the street, because one moment it was safe, and the next it was not. It had an exciting thrust.' As this reference to the zigzag walk – that curious bodily edit of urban space which we all have to practise – suggests, in many ways, that this zigzagging connects to Hadid's interest in film, wherein she sees particular affinities with architecture.

> Film is about scenario and the consequences of moving through space, but in a nonlinear manner. The fluidity of movement through film, and the way you can construct things together, and the collapse of time can really inspire architecture ... Space had been the preserve of the historicist and the postmodernist, and film helped people realise that there is another kind of space that is not historical, but is fresh and new. You go to all these underspaces and strange spaces, where fantasies are locked in

Top
Diner, New York, 2001.

Right
United Nations Headquarters Building, New York, Wallace K Harrison and others,1947–53.

Middle
Detail of United Nations Headquarters building, New York,1947–53.

the grid and which then clear the grid –
these are rather amazing things.

In the city, then, there is that cinematic
quality of not knowing what will happen next,
the jump-cut edit of city life to things that are
suddenly different – streamlined diners to great
skyscrapers or weird people doing weird things.

This New York of which Hadid speaks is also,
it has to be said, one which is disappearing. New
York today, she argues, is being 'overcleansed,
over-Disneyfied', too much like all the other
cities where urban space has become a giant
shopping precinct. She notes that, in order to
compensate perhaps, many New Yorkers are
now living out a kind of self-heightened image
of what it means to live in New York: too busy to
talk, too busy to do anything, even when they are
doing nothing. 'Ridiculous!'

Brasìlia

If New York is the place of bustle, drama and intensity, then Hadid's second city is perhaps all the more surprising given its reputation, deserved or not, for a certain sterility: Brasìlia, which she first visited in the early 1990s.

This time it is not the NY-esque density of urban life which Hadid finds intriguing. 'People always say that there is no life in Brasìlia and that is relevant, but it is not relevant to the story of Niemeyer's fixed masterplan which is like an aeroplane, which is actually not a city but the headquarters of a Catholic country.' What stimulates Hadid here, therefore, is the way in which a city can be rendered as an abstract idea of a particular country – 'Brasìlia was built in a way that was totally Brazilian: modern but not like some colonial leftover' – while pursuing a fantastically concrete architectural realisation:

'This is a city which is beautifully detailed, very abstract. Very often you see, for example, that there are no handrails, just one line here, another line there ...' For Hadid, Brasìlia represents another extreme urban condition, this time wholly different to that of New York, wherein immense national symbolism is achieved through the diagram and architectural realisations of a single architect: Oscar Niemeyer.

And, once again, one also senses a certain regret in the way in which Hadid talks about the city. But whereas for New York it was a yearning for a city that is perhaps now being lost, in the case of Brasìlia it is for a city which has yet to be truly discovered – Hadid notes that many people have never seen it outside of the few pages occasionally incorporated into architectural history texts or into style-journals like *Wallpaper**. With interest now growing in Niemeyer through new international publications and personal prizes, this situation may be about to change.

Opposite
Brasília, Cathedral and Belfry,
designed by Oscar Niemeyer,
1959, completed 1970.

Above
Brasília, National Congress,
designed by Oscar Niemeyer,
1959, completed 1960.

Moscow

Moscow is Hadid's third city, and it is perhaps the one which she mentions most often in our conversation. 'Moscow,' she explains, 'is one of the most extraordinary cities in the world.'

Once again, there are specific buildings which Hadid recalls seeing when she first visited Moscow in the late 1970s and early 1990s, especially the new kinds of building required to support the ongoing social revolution. 'I particularly remember the workers' clubs, and the idea that vertical and cultural change required not just formally new buildings but new programmes.' Here again is another realisation of the broad possibilities of architecture: that it can be responsible for the engendering of social as well as aesthetic change, and that the typology of the building may have to be invented wholly anew for these changes to occur.

But besides architectural lessons, Moscow – like New York, like Brasília – also offers its own peculiar urban conditions. The first is scale which, as Hadid describes it, is simply 'immense': 'One really doesn't realise the effect of the scale on you, because you can't tell how far away things are. Some of the skyscrapers in Moscow are basically just a projection of the towers of the Kremlin – but you cannot tell whether they are 10 metres or 10 kilometres away, because they are just so big.'

Such gestures on a city-wide scale produce 'moments of total and utter hallucination', such as the way Moscow is constructed according to an unusual visual diagram of circles. 'Concentric circles are really important: the first is the Kremlin, the next is neoclassical buildings, and then it goes into a linear park around all of Moscow, and then the housing, and then the factories – when you stand on a high point you see all this like a giant cassata.'

It is this sense of hallucination that seems to bewitch Hadid about Moscow, and she tells stories about it with a dramatic sense of her own presence and encounters. Perhaps the most vivid of these stories concerns the old outdoor Moscow swimming pool, some 200 metres across and placed in the abandoned foundations for the Palace of the Soviets:

> This place is real madness. Insane. In order to deal with the –20° or so temperature, you have to swim from indoors in order to get outdoors. Indoors, there are big fat Russian ladies watching you get changed. The showers are full of families, with huge amounts of pink flesh obscured by great clouds of steam. Then you go down into a tunnel of water, and you swim up to some glass blocks and a flap of rubber, and you just push it and you are out into the outdoor pool. Steam rises again, this time into the Moscow air. Men get their eyebrows and moustaches frozen, while still swimming ... it is the most extraordinary experience.

None of this, of course, impacts directly on Hadid's own work. There are no large open-air swimming pools, aeroplane diagrams or New York grids stamped immutably on to Hadid projects. Yet, as she explains, 'the complexity of cities and their approximate event-spaces does feed in to the quality and layout of the work. My early canvases, for example, are so jammed with information, with geometry, with an understanding of site alongside the equal importance of invention. There are so many options, and cities – all cities – give projects many other layers.' ⌂

This text is based on a conversation between Iain Borden, Helen Castle and Zaha Hadid, which took place at Zaha Hadid Architects' office in Bowling Green Lane, London, on 5 May 2001.
Iain Borden is Director of the School of Architecture at the Bartlett, UCL.

Opposite
KS Melnikov, Rusakov House of
Culture, Moscow.

Above
The Kremlin, Moscow.

Right
Palace of the Soviets, Boris
Iofan, 1930, (unrealised project).

ДВОРЕЦ СОВЕТОВ СССР

Above
Zaha Hadid, Rosenthal Center for Contemporary Art,
Cincinnati. Projected for completion in the spring of
2003, The Contemporary Arts Center is Cincinnati is
to be Hadid's most major built work to date. As such it
realises many of her ideas about the city. The design
is driven by her interpretation of the dynamism of the
project's particular urban fabric. Situated on a busy
corner site in downtown Cincinnati, it relates closely
to the movement of people within the city and reflects
the density of its cultural and urban life. This is true
of both the centre's interior and the exterior. Fully
open and glazed at street level, the interior lobby is
devised as an 'urban carpet' that simultaneously
provides a fluid continuum for existing public paths
and places and internal access to the interlocking
structure of the suspended gallery spaces. On its
exterior, the centre has two very different but
complementary facades that on the south, on Sixth
Street, is a 'dense urban bundle' of raw and heavy
volumes and on the east, on Walnut Street, takes the
form of a 'sculptural relief' that more overtly reveals
the interior composition.

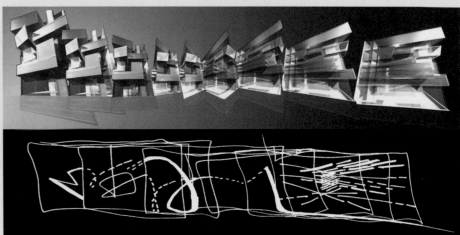

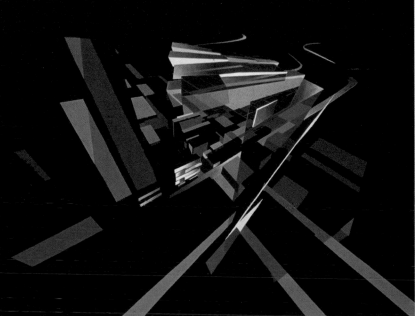

Opposite bottom
Zaha Hadid, Image and sketch
of Contemporary Arts Center,
Cincinatti.

This page
Zaha Hadid, Paintings of the
Contemporary Arts Center,
Cincinatti.

Tony Hunt

Ludic Landyacht

Since Anthony Hunt Associates was founded in 1962, Tony Hunt's firm of structural and civil engineers has collaborated on some of Britain's most seminal buildings. They include Foster Associates' Willis Faber and Dumas Building in Ipswich (1975), Michael Hopkins & Partners' Schlumberger Cambridge Research Facility and Testing Station (1985), Nicholas Grimshaw & Partners' Waterloo International Terminal in London (1993) and Future Systems' Docklands Bridge in London (1997). Most recently, the office has worked on the celebrated Eden Project in Cornwall with Nicholas Grimshaw & Partners and on the National Botanic Gardens of Wales with Foster & Partners. Rather than going for a built structure or a signature-designed product, Tony Hunt chose to discuss with Helen Castle the Ludic landyacht as his particular object of desire.

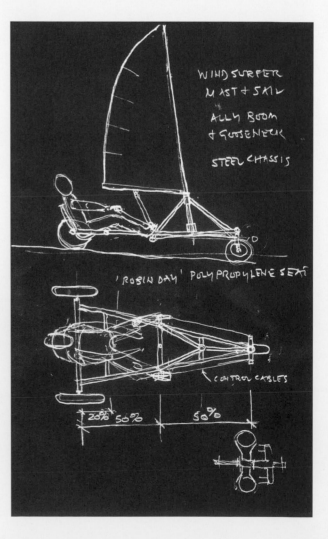

Tony Hunt's enthusiasm for the Ludic goes above and beyond that generally reserved for a pleasing designed object. Though he admires the landyacht for its simple but well-developed kit of parts, more than any thing he enjoys using it. A keen sailor, who has sailed all his life, he now lives inland a long way from the sea. The Ludic not only allows him to sail when he is confined to the *terra firma*, but also indulges his passion for speed.

Hunt is an engineer in the true sense that he likes anything that works, especially any vehicle with wheels – sports cars and motorbikes, the faster the better. He describes himself as the 'original Meccano man' who rejoices in the chance to fiddle with nuts and bolts and join things. In his youth, he put together plenty of model aircrafts; he even designed and built a control-line aeroplane while still at school. More recently, he has constructed a clockwork replica of a 1930s Mercedez Benz.

Top
Tony Hunt in front of the domes of the Eden Project, Cornwall.

Right
Sketches of the frame for Hunt's prototype for a 'sand/grass yacht'.

Opposite
The Ludic landyacht.

The Ludic is not only very fast – it goes in the region of 65 kilometres/40 miles per hour – but also has a very light construction that intensifies the sensation of speed. It is little more than a go-cart attached to a sail, its chassis very close to the ground. A precarious craft, it is steered only by the 'sailor's' feet on its pedals and it can all too easily keel over. Such a giddy sense of danger, however, only adds to the exhilaration of being dragged across the sand by a soaring wind.

Hunt first encountered landyachts when he went to France on holiday and saw them racing along the beach at Le Touquet. His imagination was fired to such an extent that on his return he seriously considered constructing his own

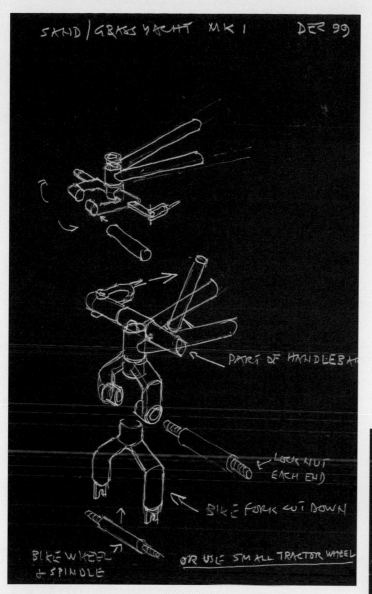

SAND/GRASS YACHT MK 1   DEC 99

PART OF HANDLEBAR

LOCK NUT
(EACH END)

BIKE FORK CUT DOWN

BIKE WHEEL
& SPINDLE

OR USE SMALL TRACTOR WHEEL

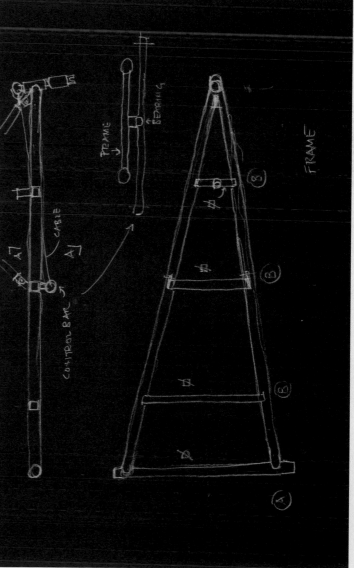

FRAME

BEARING

FRAME

CABLE

CONTROL BAR

FRAME

Opposite top
The Ludic dismantled into
a simple kit of parts: the
oxidised aluminium mast is
made up of four parts; the
three wheels unclip from the
chassis and the Dacron sail
rolls up.

Opposite middle left
The big low-pressure wheels
of the Ludic allow it to move
over fine sand.

Opposite right
Hunt constructing a model of
a 1930s Mercedez Benz racing
car. The model was issued in
kit form by the German toy
company Marklin as part of
the celebrations to mark their
75 years in business. Hunt's
wife bought the kit in Antibes
on his birthday and he
assembled it on the same day.

Top and right
Sketches of the frame
for Hunt's prototype for
a 'sand/grass yacht'.

'sand/grass yacht'. He went as far as drawing up detailed sketches for it in December 1999. He drew perspectives from the side and above and details of joints and frame; he specified a 'Robin Day' polypropylene chair for its seat, a steel chassis and a bicycle wheel, spindle and handlebars at its joints. His plans to assemble his own yacht were scuppered, however, when he encountered the Ludic. In this, he found his perfectly evolved prototype.

The Ludic is one of a range of landyachts designed and manufactured by the Breton company Seagull, which was founded more than 15 years ago by Jean-Philippe Krischer and Christine Touali. Jean-Philippe is far ahead of the game, as far as Hunt is concerned. Krischer built his first landyacht when he was only nine years old, out of a scooter fork, an exhaust pipe and a plank. By the time he started producing landyachts commercially, he had worked his way through eight prototypes. The Ludic is the Seagull's most basic and popular model,

designed for amateurs and beginners, which also comes in a scaled-down version for children. It is its perfectly engineered simplicity that makes it so satisfying for Hunt. It can be assembled and dismantled in three minutes. There are no bolts. It breaks down into six separate parts. It has a telescopic mast and the sail can be rolled up. The three separate wheels click into place. When dismantled, the yacht is small enough to go in the boot of a car and light enough to be carried by a single person. Hunt is very proud of his own yellow Ludic. It is clear that he greatly enjoys its bright sunny colour and sporty streamlined aesthetic.

Hunt has earned his unrivalled reputation in his profession for the emphasis that he places on the design element in the realisation of successful architecture. As he says of structural engineering, it is a 'mixture of art and science, in that order; concept must always come before calculation.' It is hard not to believe that he doesn't love his Ludic landyacht as much for its appearance and sense of fun – a reminder of holidays and sunnier climes – as he does for its perfected structure and mechanics. ⚐

Opposite
The Ludic shot from behind to show the single moulded body of the chassis.

Top
The lightweight yellow chassis of Hunt's Ludic.

Right
Tony Hunt on his Ludic.

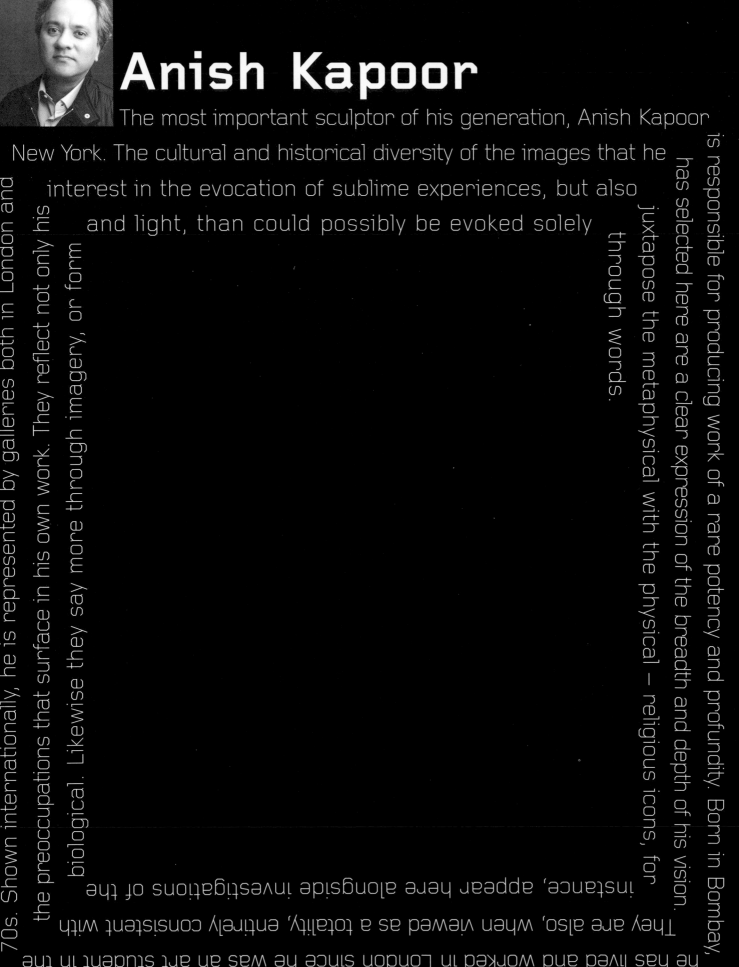

Anish Kapoor

The most important sculptor of his generation, Anish Kapoor is responsible for producing work of a rare potency and profundity. Born in Bombay, he has lived and worked in London since he was an art student in the 70s. Shown internationally, he is represented by galleries both in London and New York. The cultural and historical diversity of the images that he has selected here are a clear expression of the breadth and depth of his vision. They are also, when viewed as a totality, entirely consistent with the preoccupations that surface in his own work. They reflect not only his interest in the evocation of sublime experiences, but also juxtapose the metaphysical with the physical – religious icons, for instance, appear here alongside investigations of the biological. Likewise they say more through imagery, or form and light, than could possibly be evoked solely through words.

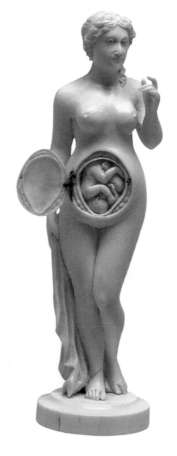

Above
Joseph Beuys, Honey Pump
at the Workplace, 1977
(Louisiana Museum of Art,
Humlebæk, Denmark).

Right
Anatomy and Pathology, 18th
or 19th century, height 160
mm, width 39 mm (Science
Museum, London). Carved
ivory anatomical figure of a
pregnant 'Venus', The
abdomen is hinged so that
when it is opened it shows
the foetus in utero.

Top
A writhing mass of snakes.

Middle left
View of the Soganli valley,
Cappadocia, Turkey.

Middle right and bottom left
Fantastic Voyage, directed by
Richard Fleischer, Twentieth
Century-Fox, 1966.

Bottom right
Jules Verne's *Journey to the
Centre of the Earth*, directed
by Henry Levin, Twentieth
Century-Fox, 1959.

Opposite top
Jose de Ribera, *La Piedad*,
c1633 (© Museo Thyssen-
Bornemisza, Madrid); oil on
canvas.

Opposite bottom
The colour red.

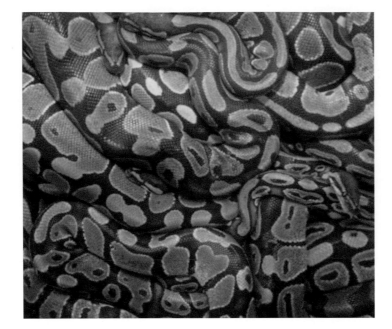

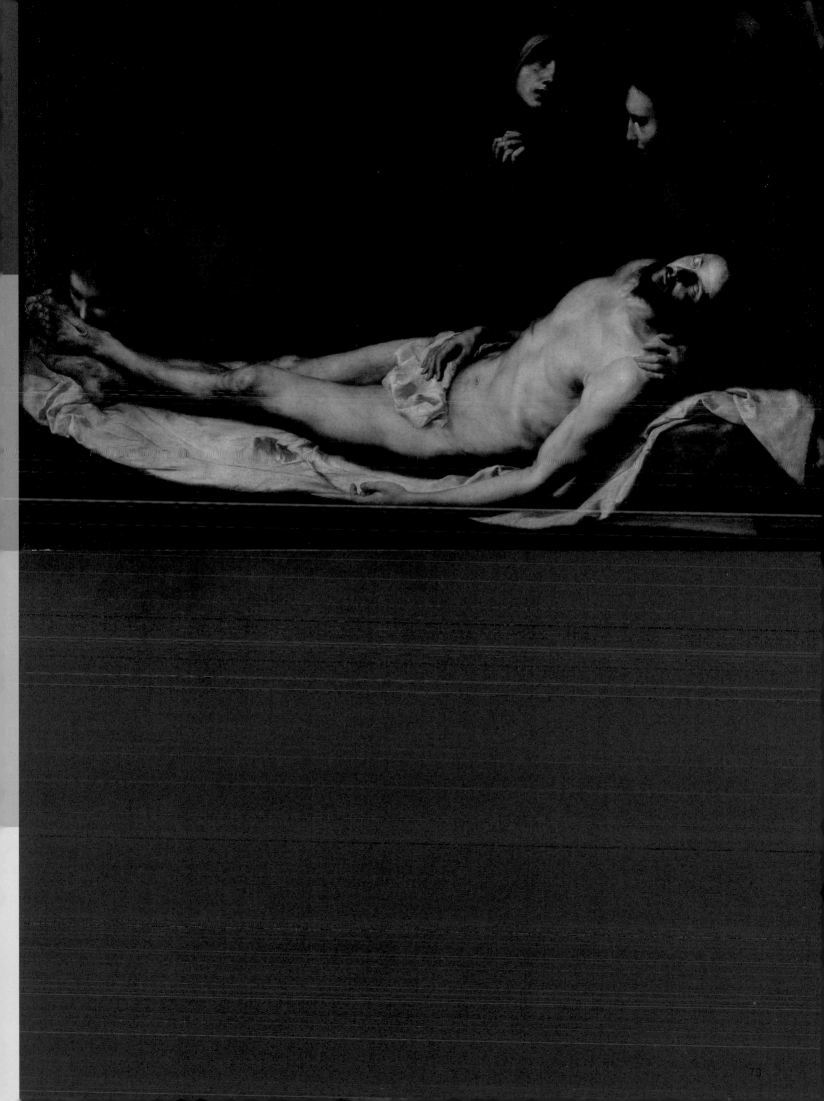

Above
Ramakrishna standing in
ecstasy during a *Kirtan* at
Keshab Chandra Sen's house
in Calcutta, 21 September
1879. Black and white print.

Right
Donatello, Sculpture of St John
the Baptist, Santa Maria
Cloriosa dei Frari, Venice.

Opposite top
Ardabil carpet (detail),
Persian, 1540 (Victoria &
Albert Museum, London).

Opposite bottom
Benares by Raghubir Singh.

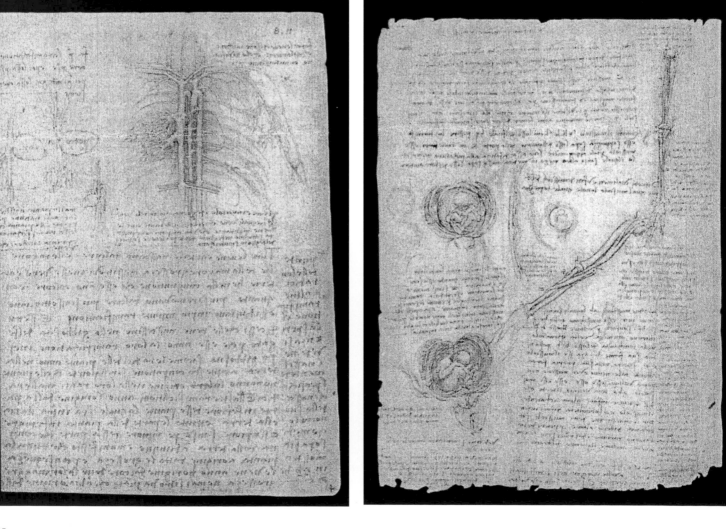

Opposite top
Ayer's Rock, Australia.

Opposite bottom
Leonardo da Vinci, *Studies of Vessels of the Thorax, the Heart and Blood Vessels: Compared with the Seed of a Plant*, c 1501 (The Royal Collection, Windsor Castle). Pen and ink on a light trace of black chalk on paper.

This page
Giovanni da Milano (c 1346–69), *Saint Francis of Assisi*, (Louvre, Paris). Oil on wood.

Ivan Margolius

1946-53

Tatra 600-Tatraplan

A Mass-Produced Teardrop Car

In his eulogy to the Tatra 600 - Tatraplan, author and architect Ivan Margolius explains how this classic Czech car was inspired by art and architecture. One of the first streamlined mass-produced cars, it was equally influenced in form by the artistic avant-garde — Constantin Brancusi's sculptures and Erich Mendelsohn's buildings — and the innovative monocoque structures of the aeronautical industry.

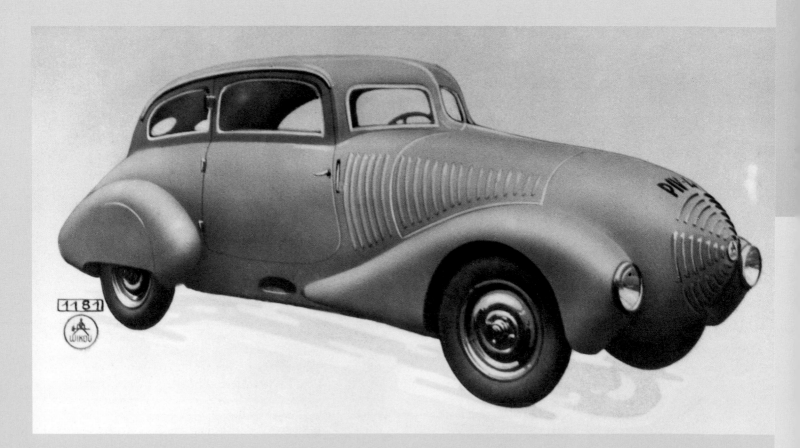

A new horizon appears. A horizon that will inspire the next phase in the evolution of the age.
—Norman Bel Geddes, *Horizons*, 1932

Take yourself back 50 years. Think of a car. Contemplate streamlining. Imagine a perfect teardrop form, the form of least resistance, on wheels. The only mass-produced automobile that fits that description would be a Tatra 600 - Tatraplan. My choice is made even easier by acknowledging that this unique automotive object was introduced in the same year in which I was born, and comes from the country of my origin – the former Czechoslovakia.

Tatra is the oldest automotive manufacturer in the world. It started in 1850 in the small Moravian town of Koprivnice making a variety of horse-drawn and, later, railway coaches. The factory was called Schustala & Co and from 1897 Koprivnice automobiles were built there. Its products were rebranded with a Tatra badge 22 years later, and innovative trucks that have been victorious in six Paris–Dakar rallies are still produced there.

Why is the Tatraplan so memorable and such a milestone in automotive design evolution? It came as the end result of a line of revolutionary developments in streamlining which Tatra bravely attempted, and had an innovative monocoque body construction. Encouraged by the progress in Zeppelin design, early Junkers

and Dornier aeroplanes, studies of natural forms by D'Arcy Wentworth Thompson in his book *On Growth and Form* (1917) and new expression in Constantin Brancusi's art and the architecture of Erich Mendelsohn, the science of aerodynamics became established. In developing automobile design, it was realised that in order to consume less fuel and achieve greater speed and power it was necessary to consider improving air penetration.

Hungarian Paul Jaray, the main advocate of aerodynamics, who lived and worked in Switzerland, obtained several patents for streamlined car bodies in the 1920s. In 1931 the Czech company Wikow produced a car called Kapka (meaning 'drop') that attempted a streamlined form. Progress was accelerated for racing and experimental cars and streamlining was applied in a number of cases. However, the general public taste was against such a radical departure from the established cubic forms of vehicles and it was only in the mid-1930s that car manufacturers attempted to market streamlined cars. The Czech Tatra was such a pioneer.

In 1897 Hans Ledwinka (1878–1967), an Austrian by birth, had begun to work in the Koprivnice factory and his bold approach soon led him to the directorship of the automobile division. He introduced swing axles attached to a central tubular chassis that was powered

Opposite top
Ivan Margolius in the Czech
Republic with
his 1949 Tatraplan.

Opposite bottom
Wikow Kapka, 1931.

Above
Tatra 77, 1934.

by a front air-cooled engine. This arrangement
provided a very flexible framework that became
proven and successful on the rough Central
European roads.

In 1933 Ledwinka, with Erich Uebelacker,
designed the model T77, a large fully
streamlined car with a rear air-cooled engine,
that created a sensation when it was exhibited at
the Berlin Autosalon. The single stabilising fin on
its rear became a Tatra trademark. In the next
year mass production followed and additional
streamlined models – the T77a (1935), T87 (1936)
and T97 (1937) – came on the market.

These designs were, however, a step back
from a full streamlined form as they expressed
the front wings separately from the main body.
This is where the postwar Tatraplan succeeded.
Its body, a teardrop form, fully enclosed the
chassis and the wheels, wide at the front over
the wheels with a sloping split-windscreen and
the back dissected by a small, almost symbolic,
fin sweeping to the pointed rear lid.

The Tatraplan had a stormy and adventurous
beginning. After the Second World War, Tatra
wanted to bring a new design to the market that
would continue the tradition of streamlined
models and at the same time achieve greater
improvement in comfort. The goals were to
lower the overall weight, distribute it evenly over

Opposite top
Tatra 77a, 1935.

Opposite bottom
Tatra 87, 1936.

Above
Tatra 97, 1937.

the chassis, increase the interior space, design a body with the smallest drag coefficient, improve operational economy and introduce an all-metal body. The new model was to be based on the prewar Tatra 97, designed by Hans Ledwinka and his son Erich, of which only 508 cars were built before the occupying Third Reich stopped its production because of its closeness to the KdF-Wagen (Volkswagen).

With Hans Ledwinka in prison, gaoled for alleged and unproved collaboration during the war (he was released in 1951 and fully rehabilitated in 1992), the factory was left without a strong designer. The chief engineer, Julius Mackerle, who replaced Ledwinka, appointed engineer Cvetnic to take on the role. Initially Cvetnic proposed to modernise the T97 model. This was not accepted. Then came

Professor Soucek under whose leadership a new car began to emerge. Josef Chalupa, director of the body design department, proposed the concept of a self-supporting steel monocoque streamlined body (years ahead of what was being developed in the rest of the world) with a flat punt-type frame with perforated welded-box side members and a central rib that forked into a Y-form at the rear to accept a new air-cooled, horizontally opposed, four-cylinder engine mounted on two radial silentblocs. The first prototype was completed in December 1946. However, the tests which followed found bad stability, inadequate power, and poor engine cooling and interior heating. The second prototype, made in spring 1947, did not solve any of these problems and Soucek departed.

Engineer Korbel, assisted by Vladimir Popelar, was asked to build five prototypes for the Prague Autosalon in autumn 1947. To find the best way forward Popelar

Ons plan.... een

Tatraplan

AUTO PALACE ʼS GRAVENHAGE

TATRAPLAN

Tatraplan

and Chalupa arranged a meeting with Ledwinka, through his former chauffeur, to obtain his advice. In May 1947, at midnight, they came to see Ledwinka in his prison cell bringing all the drawings of the new car with them. Ledwinka welcomed them with open arms and after a 2 ½ hour consultation gave his views. He liked the form of the car but suggested enlarging the engine capacity, redesigning the engine fan-cooling arrangement and rear axle assembly, moving the headlights from the bonnet to the edge of the front wings, introducing roof cooling vents and keeping the traditional Tatra rear fin which was missing on the prototypes.

The new cars were delivered to the autosalon with hours to spare and were a widely acclaimed success. When tested in a wind tunnel, the Tatraplan – its name implies a connection to a contemporary two-year economic 'plan' as well the fact that its streamlining was inspired by aeroplanes (colloquial. Czech: ero'plan') – had an impressive 0.32 drag coefficient. The Tatraplans were triumphant in a number of rallies, especially in the 1949 Osterreichische Alpenfahrt where they gained the first four places. By the beginning of 1953, 6,342 units had been produced, a third of which were exported into 17 countries but not into the UK.

Tatra was the only company that faithfully embraced streamlining principles and was the first to bring them into mass production. Individual experiments carried out by others such as Jenatzy's La Jamais Contente (1899), Conte Ricotti's Alfa Romeo by Castagna (1913), Rumpler's Tropfen-Auto (1921), Jaray's Ley (1922), Audi (1923), Dixi (1923) and Burney's Streamliner (1930) paved the way for its achievement. The line of Tatra teardrop streamlined cars created a benchmark for the future development of the automobile.

Last year I fulfilled my dream when I bought a Tatraplan made in 1949. After some restoration I am looking forward to racing against the wind along the roads, and paying tribute to the pioneering spirit of automobile design and its forgotten heroes. ⌂

Ivan Margolius is the author of Automobiles by Architects (Wiley-Academy), 2000.

Opposite top left
Tatraplan: Dutch
advertisement, 1951.

Opposite top right
Tatraplan promotional
material, 1951.

Opposite bottom
Contemporary advertisement,
1948.

Above
Tatraplan brochure cover,
1948.

Right
25th International Jubilee
Motor Show poster, Prague,
1935.

Contributors Biographies

Ron Arad

The son of a painter mother and photographer father, Ron Arad was born in Tel Aviv, Israel, in 1951. After studying at the Jerusalem Academy of Art, he attended the Architectural Association in London. In 1981, he established One Off Ltd with Caroline Thorman. Well-known early pieces include: the 'Rover Chair', the 'Transformer' chair and the remote-controlled 'Aerial' light. In 1989, he founded Ron Arad Associates with Thorman. In 1997 he was appointed Professor of Furniture Design at the Royal College of Art in London. He is now the RCA's Professor of Product Design. Architectural commissions include: the foyer for the new Tel Aviv Opera House, and the Belgo restaurants in London.

Klaus Bode

Klaus Bode is the Director of BDSP Partnership, the consulting engineers. He has a BSc (Hons) in building engineering from the University of Bath. Before founding BDSP in 1995 with his fellow partners, he worked for J Roger and Preston and Partners and RP & K Sozietät. BDSP Partnership collaborated with Future Systems on the APAS environmental research and development project, Project Zed (Zero Emission Design) including a number of other 'low energy' projects. Examples of current BDSP projects include Richard Rogers Partnership's National Assembly for Wales, a hotel and the conversion of a bullring into a recreational centre in Barcelona, the Pritzker Tower in Chicago and research work in harnessing wind energy in an urban context.

Borge Boeskov

Borge Boeskov is the President of Boeing Business Jets. In 1996 Boeing and General Electric joined forces to produce the Boeing Business Jet. Under the leadership of Boeing Business Jets' President Borge Boeskov, BBJ sales have far surpassed original predictions. Boeskov, a native of Iceland, first joined Boeing in 1965. In 1997 he was chosen by *Aviation Week & Space Technology* magazine as one of its 1997 aerospace laureates for his outstanding achievements.

Brian Clarke

The architectural artist Brian Clarke has been responsible for some of the most enduring and radical stained-glass windows of the last 25 years, including the recent Al Faisaliah Centre in Riyadh, the Pfizer world headquarters in New York and the Swiss Bank cone in Connecticut. Lord Foster has described Clarke as, 'one of those very few artists who understands the spatial world of architecture – the core issues of space and light.' Clarke's paintings and architectural projects in stained glass, mosaic and tapestry can be found all over the world. Born in 1953 in Lancashire, England, Clarke presently lives London, Munich and New York.

Peter Cook

Since 1990 Peter Cook has been Bartlett Professor and Head of Architecture at University College London. A founding member of Archigram, Cook started the 'Archigram' pamphlet in 1961 with David Greene and Michael Webb, and went on to form the Archigram Group with Ron Herron, Warren Chalk and Dennis Crompton. Cook's extensive teaching activities commenced in 1964 at the Architectural Association in London. In 1984, previous to his post as Bartlett Professor at UCL, he was also appointed Professor and Head of the Architecture Faculty at the HBK 'Staedelschule', Frankfurt. In 1976, Cook formed an office with Professor Christine Hawley, with whom he is now working on public housing in various countries and on the Museum of Antiquities in Lower Austria. In 2000, Cook and Colin Fournier won the international competition for the Kunsthaus in Graz. Cook is currently contracted to design the extension of the town of Pinto (near Madrid) and is exhibiting his latest work at FORM ZERO, Santa Monica, California.

Kathryn Gustafson

Kathryn Gustafson has over 20 years of experience in landscape design and is a principal of Gustafson Porter in London and Gustafson Partners Ltd in Seattle. The work of both offices emphasises the sculptural qualities of site-specific, contextual landscape design. Until 1995, when Gustafson started gaining major commissions in the rest of Europe and the United States, Gustafson's highly renowned work was largely confined to France. The setting up of the London and Seattle offices has allowed the design approach of her earlier work to evolve in response to new contexts of time, culture and location.

Projects have ranged in scale from one to 60 hectacres, in both urban and rural settings. Recent projects include: the Arthur Ross Terrace at the American Museum of Natural History in New York; the great glasshouse al the National Botanic Garden of Wales, with Foster and Partners; a 15-hectare cultural park for the city of Amsterdam; the Seattle Civic Center; the Garden of Imagination in Terrasson, France; and Seattle's Marion Oliver McCaw Hall, with LMN Architects. In Europe Kathryn is currently working in collaboration with Neil Porter on a civic space for Swiss Cottage in north London.

Kathryn Gustafson is an honorary fellow of the Royal Institute of British Architects, a medallist of the French Academy of Architecture and the recipient of London's Jane Drew Prize. She is an active lecturer and is published internationally.

Zaha Hadid

Born in Baghdad, Zaha Hadid studied architecture at the Architectural Association in London, where she taught until 1987. After winning the Diploma Prize in 1977, Hadid joined the Office for Metropolitan Architecture. In 1979, she set up her own practice and soon came to prominence, winning the Architectural Design Gold Medal with her design for 59 Eaton Place, London. She has gained first place in many international competitions, including those for The Peak Club, Hong Kong (1986) and Kufürstendamm, Berlin (1986); for an art and media centre in Düsseldorf (1989); and for the Cardiff Bay Opera House (1994). Other projects have included furniture and interiors for Bitar, London (1985), and the design of several buildings in Japan including two projects in Tokyo (1988) and a folly in Osaka (1990). In 1990, Hadid received the commission for the Vitra fire station in Weil am Rhein. She is currently working on a large portfolio of projects, including the third bridge crossing, Abu Dhabi; the Strasbourg tram station; the Contemporary Arts Center, Cincinnati; and the Contemporary Arts Centre, Rome. Hadid's paintings and drawings have been shown internationally. Major exhibitions include the Guggenheim Museum, New York (1978); the Museum of Modern Art, New York (1988); The Graduate School of Design at Harvard University (1994); and the ICA, London (2000).

Anthony Hunt

Since Tony Hunt founded Anthony Hunt Associates in 1962 it has developed into a premier engineering-design group, working with leading British architects. First and foremost a designer, Hunt believes in creating a structure that is in sympathy with the architect's concept, while at the same time having its own structural integrity, and is actively involved in the design development of projects. He has lectured extensively at universities in the USA and Europe and holds the Graham Willis Professor Visiting Chair in Architecture at Sheffield University. He is the author of a number of articles and books, including *Tony Hunt's Structures Notebook* and *Tony Hunt's Sketchbook*.

Jan Kaplicky

Jan Kaplicky is the founding principal of the innovative London-based practice Future Systems. Its most renowned buildings to date are the Hauer-King House, London, which had two television documentaries and a monograph devoted to it; and the NatWest Media Centre at Lord's Cricket Ground, London, which received the 1999 Stirling Prize. Future Systems has also captured the imagination with a series of exciting shops for Comme Des Garçons and Marni. The office is currently completing a new Selfridges department store for Birmingham, England. Born in Prague, Czechoslovakia, Kaplicky came to London in 1968. Before founding Future Systems in 1979, he worked for Denys Lasdun, Piano & Rogers, Spencer & Webster and Foster Associates. He is now in partnership at Future Systems with his wife, Amanda Levette.

Anish Kapoor

Anish Kapoor is one of the most influential sculptors of his generation. Born in Bombay, India, he has lived and worked in London since the early 1970s. His work has been exhibited worldwide and is held in numerous private and public collections including the Tate Gallery, the Museum of Modern Art in New York, the Reina Sofia in Madrid and the Stedlijk Museum in Amsterdam. He was awarded the Premio 2000 in 1990, when he was represented in the British Pavilion at the Venice Biennale. In 1991, he won the Turner Prize. For more on his work, see www.lisson.co.uk

Ivan Margolius

Ivan Margolius is an architect and the author of a number of articles and books on architecture, design and automobiles including *Tatra – The Legacy of Hans Ledwinka* (1990), *Skoda Laurin & Klement* (1992), *Prague – a guide to twentieth-century architecture* (1994, 1996) and *Automobiles by Architects* (2000).

Multi-Source Synthesis: Engaging Pre-Engineering Technology in Chongqing, China

Developing a dynamic dialogue between macro and micro scales in the production of a sustainable masterplan

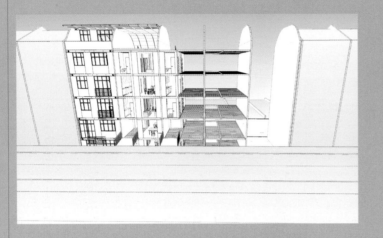

The British engineering consultancy Battle McCarthy is internationally renowned for its proactive promotion and production of high-quality, sustainable design. From 1994 to 1997, the practice explored the potential of sustainability through 'Multi-Source Synthesis', a series of ground-breaking, theoretical articles in *Architectural Design*, which will be published in anthology form by Wiley-Academy in autumn 2001. It is, however, the office's unique emphasis on innovative research and development, coupled with years of experience of designing sophisticated green projects, that has given them such a comprehensive understanding of sustainable issues. As a prologue to the long-running 'Multi-Source Synthesis' series, *AD Plus* features here a new project by Battle McCarthy which is set to revolutionise housing on a global scale through its evolution of a sustainable building technology.

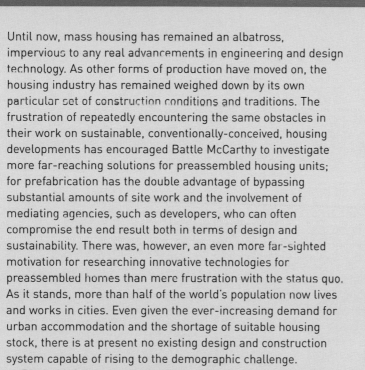

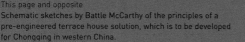

Above
Map of western China, showing Chongqing, the proposed site of ECOS.
A housing project on a massive, unpredented scale, it can only be
realised by using the pre-engineering technology that Battle McCarthy
are helping to develop.

This page and opposite
Schematic sketches by Battle McCarthy of the principles of a
pre-engineered terrace house solution, which is to be developed
for Chongqing in western China.

Until now, mass housing has remained an albatross, impervious to any real advancements in engineering and design technology. As other forms of production have moved on, the housing industry has remained weighed down by its own particular set of construction conditions and traditions. The frustration of repeatedly encountering the same obstacles in their work on sustainable, conventionally-conceived, housing developments has encouraged Battle McCarthy to investigate more far-reaching solutions for preassembled housing units; for prefabrication has the double advantage of bypassing substantial amounts of site work and the involvement of mediating agencies, such as developers, who can often compromise the end result both in terms of design and sustainability. There was, however, an even more far-sighted motivation for researching innovative technologies for preassembled homes than mere frustration with the status quo. As it stands, more than half of the world's population now lives and works in cities. Even given the ever-increasing demand for urban accommodation and the shortage of suitable housing stock, there is at present no existing design and construction system capable of rising to the demographic challenge.

Battle McCarthy are proposing the proliferation of a wholly new sustainable building technology that could usher in a new era of residential urban environmental building design, with major global consequences. It is a system of preassembled housing that is set to transform 20th-century preconceptions of modular construction. Whereas in previous decades prefabrication has been associated with the lowest common denominator of social housing and ultimately with 'failed' construction techniques, the proposed system is to be precision-engineered to a high quality at a reasonable cost. This should not only allow environmental building technology to infiltrate the construction industry in a way that is inconceivable at present, but also ultimately allow it to saturate the market unchallenged.

Though Battle McCarthy have been developing this building technology through their work on some of the largest housing schemes in Britain – such as the Greenwich Millennium Village

and the Elephant and Castle in London – the next stage in its evolution has been dependent on their engagement on a project substantial enough to require a dedicated manufacturing base. (Within Europe, for instance, housing is not on a large enough scale to warrant the establishment of such a base.) However, the new housing construction programme in western China, on which they have been invited to collaborate along with the Chongqing Construction Commission, Chongqing University and Hong Kong Polytechnic, has been set up to rehouse a million people made homeless by the Three Gorges Dam project and the flooding of the Yangtze River. Entitled ECOS, this innovative scheme of industrial housing will produce precison-engineered and advanced IT-configured homes that will be applicable locally and globally. For, once it has been established, the ECOS's manufacturing base will export houses for a full range of international uses including, for example, the provision of key workers' accommodation in London.

Four major factors make Chongqing ripe for the implementation of ECOS: the current and potential wealth of the region; the urgent need for a major construction programme; the government's concerns over the environmental impact of proposed construction; and the existence of a local shipbuilding industry with relevant skills for producing prefabricated housing units.

Chongqing Municipality

Chongqing is a rapidly developing area based along the upper reaches of the Yangtze River. China's largest municipality, it is based at the heart of the Three Gorges project, which is the world's largest flood-control dam and hydroelectric project. The greater area is home to 30 million people with a population density of 367 people per square kilometre. Chongqing has a wealth of natural resources and provides a vast market potential for future development. A new infrastructure is beginning to evolve that will need to meet the investment demands

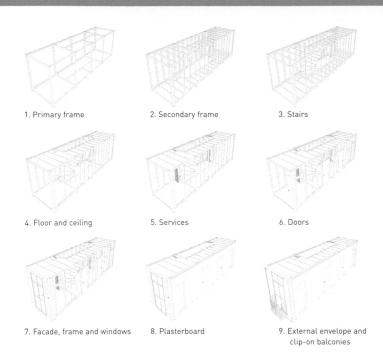

1. Primary frame
2. Secondary frame
3. Stairs
4. Floor and ceiling
5. Services
6. Doors
7. Facade, frame and windows
8. Plasterboard
9. External envelope and clip-on balconies

and consumption needs of the millions of people who are now cultivating a good standard of living. The municipality has the resources and is ideally situated for the implementation of the ECOS system, with population densities that make mass production a necessary element of the process.

Future Housing Demand in Chongqing

The Chinese central and regional governments have conducted studies that reveal the need for Chongqing to undergo a major construction programme in order to meet future housing demands. It has been forecast that this will require the construction of 61,500,000 square metres of living space within the next five years. This increased demand has been caused by a number of factors, including the migration of people from rural to urban areas and the displacement and relocation of one million people due to the Three Gorges Dam Project.

The space demands per person in Chongqing are also increasing. In 1978, it was three square metres per person and this doubled within 16 years to 6.3 square metres per person in 1994. It is now estimated to be eight square metres per person and is expected to reach 12 square metres per person by 2005. The ECOS system can meet this challenge by providing a building system that can be erected quickly and efficiently and will be able to respond to the growth in space demands as the quality of life in China grows.

The Environmental Impact of Proposed Construction

At present China produces only four times the amount of electricity generated in the UK for 20 times as many people. A person living in China produces around one tonne of CO_2 per year while an average American 'emits' 20 tonnes. These numbers could change dramatically in China as the standard of living increases and the demand for better lifestyles intensifies. The central and local governments recognise this and are extremely concerned about the environmental impact of proposed construction programmes, not only in Chongqing but also throughout China. In response, they are establishing sustainability targets that are no different to significant redevelopments in major Western cities. These will include environmental strategies that make use of available funding through carbon trading initiatives and that focus on construction quality, energy, water, waste and IT management. Chongqing is exploring industrialised housing (as is the UK) as a way to meet local as well as international environmental objectives. The ecologically and environmentally advanced designs of the ECOS system will help to establish the infrastructures necessary to address the short- and long-term environmental issues that will arise. The design includes rainwater harvesting and recycling, low energy input during construction, zero CO_2 emission, renewable energy, effective waste management and recycling, low maintenance, high insulation and air tightness, as well as demountable and reusable structures and services.

Industrialised Housing

Industrialised housing to replace poor-quality traditional construction has become the development policy in Chongqing. It uses the same manufacturing techniques as the local shipbuilding industry, which produces passenger liners (including cabin fit-out) as well as shops and major infrastructure and industrial components such as bridges and manufacturing plants. Chongqing has the local resources to implement the housing construction programme, but accepts the need to import international design expertise and appropriate equipment to adapt its shipbuilding industry. To this end, Battle McCarthy has developed the scheme design for a pre-engineered town-house system aimed at the middle-income and high-density inner-city market. The combination of the manufacturing techniques of China with the designs of Battle McCarthy will result in the precision-engineered mass production of large numbers of units. These numbers would have never been achievable in the West as the populations are not as extreme. This provides the ideal opportunity to demonstrate the benefits of the ECOS system to the housing industry in the West where industrialised housing is not a financially viable option.

Pre-Engineered Solutions

The pre-engineered town-house system is constructed from six stacked 'wet' units that incorporate kitchen and bathroom zones as well as a stair core. These are precommissioned, and entirely manufactured off site with the floor and roof units. Everything is produced in a precision-engineering environment using low-embodied-energy recycled materials. All elements are

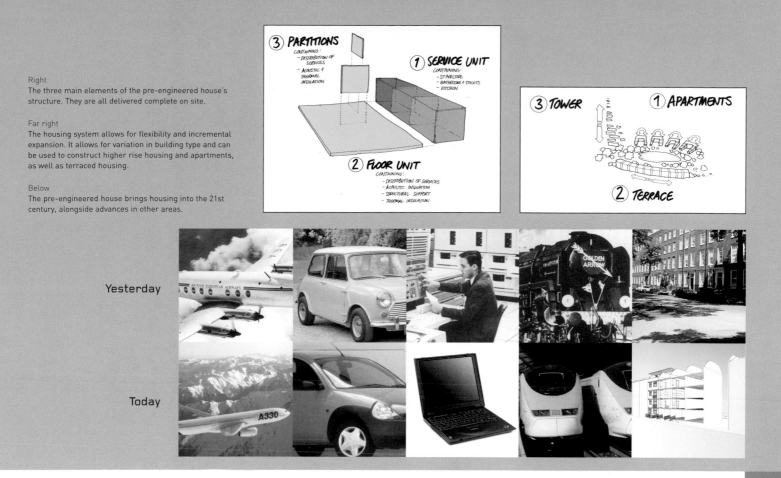

delivered completed in the largest finished units and are assembled on the site where they create a full-span structure that allows for flexibility and incremental expansion.

Pre-engineered housing is environmentally streamlined with zero defects in order to maximise efficiency and achieve zero CO_2 emissions. The town house is also an intelligent/smart home that possesses a computerised building control/management system and incorporates advanced features such as 'central locking' and home care or medical health monitoring.

Joined-Up Thinking and the Benefits to the Community

Quality and affordable IT-configured homes have obvious direct benefits for the housing industry but, in addition, the ECOS project has far-reaching benefits such as:

Transportation – IT links to public transport
Education – IT lifetime learning
Health – Quality environment
Retail – Centralised locking that provides controlled access
Social security – Home-care facilities for the elderly and infirm
Employment – Quality construction and dual-use homes

No longer can housing be isolated from the government departments of health, education, transportation, employment, energy, social security and the environment. Although it is a small government budget compared to those for other community needs, it has a major influence on the performance of other departments. The treasury has already made moves to escalate best-practice guidelines, which will be extended to include all the benefits mentioned above.

Summary

The success of this partnership between Battle McCarthy and developers in China will provide a workable solution for growth

there, as well as demonstrating to the house-building industry in the West that precision engineering is necessary to manufacture large numbers of preassembled homes. Designs can then be applied to the increased urban development currently taking place in London and other international cities. The sustainable building techniques developed by Battle McCarthy will provide economic and best-value benefits as well as 'future proofing' the system for the expected developments in renewable energy systems.

Battle McCarthy recognise the value of the opportunities that global sustainability will bring to the housing industry, and hope this will soon be recognised by multinationals as low-energy industrial housing manufactured in China becomes a market opportunity both overseas and at home. In the near future, a superior industrialised home may be imported from Chongqing to provide a significantly better product than traditional housing, with all the intelligent home facilities for the same price as a minimum-specification home in the UK. Ideally, a housing factory can be built on the outskirts of any major city, providing necessary quality housing wherever it is needed.

Battle McCarthy is a visionary practice that realises the necessity for sustainable engineering design in architecture. The ECOS project represents a significant step in the realisation of a high-quality and practical system for environmental housing. The practice has discovered the technology for saving the planet and preventing our own self-destruction. Now it will be applied on an unimaginable scale. ∆

Gigon/Guyer

In the first few years of their practice, the Swiss architects Gigon/Guyer designed buildings for three major art museums. Since then their work has shifted from being concerned solely with displaying art to also making art – they have collaborated with artists and landscape artists on a number of commissions. Annette LeCuyer describes the extraordinary output of this office, which is underpinned by a fascination with materials that succeeds in being precise and experimental, and at the same time sensuous.

Opposite bottom left
The exhibition rooms at the Kirchner Museum, Davos, 1992. In the museum the architects used glass in a variety of different ways: unexpectedly, as with the translucent glass that clads the insulated concrete walls of the exhibition rooms; and in more familiar ways, as with the translucent glazing of the 'light rooms' above the gallery spaces.

Opposite bottom right
Museum of Art extension, Winterthur, 1995. Here Gigon and Guyer's preoccupation with glass, first established at the Kirchner Museum, is extended. Industrial glass planks are combined with industrial galvanised-steel insulation trays to create an exquisite, mercurial building envelope.

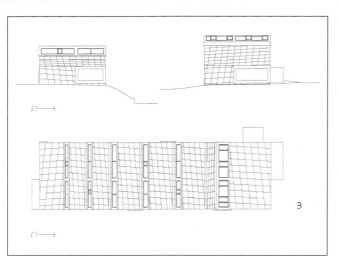

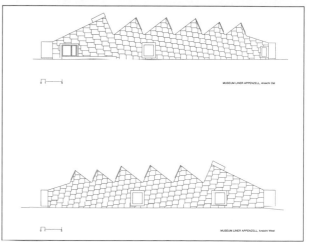

The Kirchner Museum, set in the resort town of Davos high in the Swiss Alps, was designed to house the works of the German Expressionist painter Ernst Ludwig Kirchner. The scheme was selected as the winner of an architectural competition in 1989, and the completed museum opened three years later. It is an accomplished building by any standard. That it was the first completed project designed by the architects Gigon/Guyer makes it all the more outstanding. In place of the sophomoric flourish that often characterises the first works of young offices, it was the mature, quiet restraint of the Kirchner Museum that attracted international attention and critical acclaim.

Annette Gigon and Mike Guyer met at the Federal Institute of Technology (ETH) in Zurich. Following completion of their studies in 1984, Annette worked with Herzog & de Meuron in Basel and Mike joined Rem Koolhaas in the Office of Metropolitan Architecture in Rotterdam. From the founding of their own office in 1989, the development of Gigon/Guyer's work has been sure-footed. Many of their commissions have resulted from successful competition entries, and the completed projects have won numerous awards in Switzerland and Italy. Their extension to the Museum of Art in Winterthur

Liner Museum, Appenzell, 1998.
Designed to house the work of two artists – Carl Liner, father and son – the museum is located at the edge of a small historic town. The plan is comprised of a series of small exhibition rooms with north-facing skylights. Orientation is provided by windows looking east and west, and by large oriel-like projections at each end of the building. Sheet chrome-steel cladding, sandblasted to diffuse light, is used on both the roof and facade giving the building a monolithic character.

Top left
Roof plan of the Liner Museum.

Bottom right
East and west elevations of the Liner Museum.

Top right
Exterior of the Liner Museum.

Bottom left
The exterior of the Liner Museum is clad with sandblasted, sheet chrome-steel shingles.

Signal box, Zurich, 1999.
Located at the edge of Zurich, the building houses
electronic switchgear for the Swiss Federal Railway.
Technical facilities and computer security systems are
on the lower levels with control rooms on the top floor
overlooking the tracks. In contrast with the reflective
metallised glazing of the control room windows, iron-
oxide pigment in the concrete integrates the building
into its surroundings – indeed almost camouflages it.

Above
The signal box.

Right
The signal box blends into its industrial surroundings.

was nominated for the prestigious Mies van der Rohe Award
for European Architecture in 1996 and, two years later, the
Liner Museum in Appenzell was shortlisted for the same
award.

When they were first invited to exhibit their work in Lucerne
in 1993, Gigon/Guyer had completed only two buildings.
However, titling the exhibition 'Werkstoff' (material) at the
Architekturgalerie, Lucerne, provided an opportunity for them
to show samples of the components they had used to help
them initially visualise, and then construct, their projects. Laid
out like the ingredients of a recipe or the equipment for a
laboratory experiment, the exhibition made the obvious point
that materials can be combined in many ways to make
different buildings. It also stressed the focus of Gigon/Guyer
upon the development of a precise, minimal material grammar
that endows ordinary building materials with new visual
meaning and heightened sensory and sensual impact. The
Kirchner Museum, for example, is an essay that explores the
potential of glass, that most ubiquitous of modern building
materials. At Davos, Gigon/Guyer have used it in expected ways
for its transparent and translucent qualities but also
unexpectedly, as cladding to concrete and, in pellet form, as
roof ballast. Their subsequent design for a new gallery addition
to the Winterthur Museum, completed in 1995, extends those
studies by combining industrial glass planks with galvanised-
steel insulation trays to create an exquisite, mercurial building
envelope.

Although their 1998 Liner Museum in Appenzell
remained focused upon the development of a material
grammar, here Gigon/Guyer have pursued a slightly
different strategy. Instead of using material in an
unexpected context, they use flat metal sheet quite
conventionally as a cladding system, but manipulate
it visually. What initially appears to be an ordinary
industrial metal shed with a sawtooth roof is revealed,
upon closer inspection, to be a subtle exercise in
proportion and perspective. In place of identical
repeated bays, the building is composed of a series
of modules that decrease in plan and sectional
dimensions from south to north, a progression that
is reiterated by the decreasing size of the sheet metal
shingles.

Because of their numerous museum commissions,
much of the work of Gigon/Guyer has inevitably
concentrated upon the creation of architecture to house
art. In these circumstances, they have been careful to
keep art and architecture separate and to downplay
architecture for the sake of the art. However, on recent
projects for a wide range of uses including housing,
recreation and industry, they have sought out artists
to work with them to make architecture. These
collaborations have led Gigon/Guyer into explorations
in the use of colour, both applied and integral. This
interest in colour, advanced alongside considerations

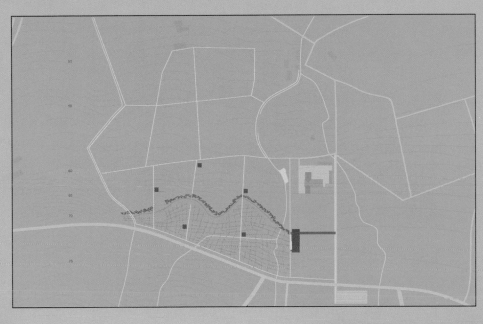

Museum and Archaeological Park, Kalkriese, 2000
The park is designed to focus visitors' attention not only on a famous battle between the Romans and the ancient Germans, but also on the present. Together with a museum housing archaeological findings and a series of pavilions in the park, the landscape is designed to reveal evidence of the marks of culture, both peaceful and violent, imposed on the site over the centuries.

Above left
Site plan of the Archaeological Park.

Left and below
Sections of the Listening, Seeing and Understanding Pavilions at Kalkriese.

Following page:
Top, left and right
The Listening Pavilion.

Middle, left and right
The Seeing Pavilion.

Bottom, left and right
The Understanding Pavilion.

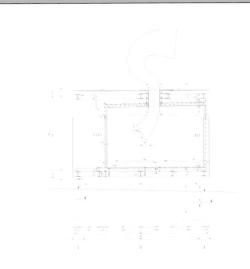

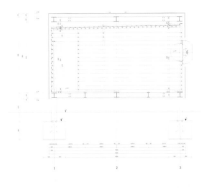

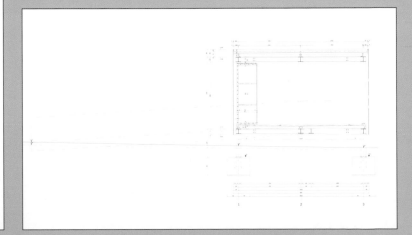

of material quality, has led them to exploit the potential of matter to transform over time. Although weathering is by no means a new architectural concern, Gigon/Guyer engage it as a positive, rather than negative, agent of change. In their design for a new signal box in Zurich, they have taken their inspiration from the patina of iron dust, released by train brakes, that covers everything along the tracks. By incorporating iron-oxide pigment in the concrete mix, the static, dull grey material character of concrete is replaced by a rich, evolving mix of hues from yellow and orange to deep purple. Through what Gigon/Guyer like to call 'alchemy', the

flat surface of the concrete becomes deep and, as the iron pigment rusts, the building changes from day to day and in response to weather and light conditions.

For their most recent project – a museum and archaeological park at Kalkriese in Germany won in an international design competition– Gigon/Guyer have collaborated with landscape artists and archaeologists to explore time through the material character of landscape. The museum and park are designed to explain where and how the Varus battle between the ancient Germans and the Romans took place in 9AD.

Within the framework of a new landscape plan for the site, three different pathway systems are overlaid to document human impact on the land. Steel paving slabs mark the route of the Roman legions. Inscribed with text, numbers and symbols relating to events on the site, the slabs are placed irregularly to denote the chaos of battle. Carefully aligned steel poles mark the position and height of the earthwork defences constructed by the Germans, and a network of narrow woodchip paths in the forest enables visitors to experience the freedom of movement the Germans enjoyed behind the earthworks. A further system of gravel paths marks the recent agricultural use of the land.

A reconstruction of the landscape of the battle – forest, clearing and marsh – is excavated into the ground. Visitors descend into the reconstructed landscape on ramps along steel-sheet-pile retaining walls inscribed with a full scale section explaining the layers of soil that have accumulated over time. Along the Roman path, three steel-clad pavilions – Listening, Seeing and Understanding – are designed to heighten the sensory impact of the landscape and to connect the idea of conflict with more peaceful patterns of land use. In contrast with the battle site, the museum building is lifted above the ground. Located at the entrance to the park, it is clad with weathering steel panels externally and black untreated steel internally. After entering a horizontal volume with an auditorium and exhibition space, visitors move up through a vertical volume that houses open-air exhibition areas and culminates in an observation deck overlooking the park and its surroundings.

The entire project – museum, pavilions, paths, poles and sunken landscape – is defined by a single material, steel, that is differentiated only by a range of oiled, painted and weathering finishes. Gigon/Guyer's transformation of the perception of material through juxtaposition, time and heightened sensual awareness is artfully marshalled to elucidate the cultural landscape of Kalkriese. With this project, Gigon/Guyer's preoccupations have expanded from the individual building in its immediate context to a larger and more complex physical, cultural and temporal setting. Yet, even at this greater scale, the simplicity and careful restraint of their work remains potent – a welcome respite from the excess of much contemporary architecture, and a hopeful sign that the territory they are exploring will continue to yield fertile contributions to architectural discourse. ⌂

Annette LeCuyer is an architect and an associate professor at the University of Michigan. She is author of *Radical Tectonics* (Thames and Hudson, 2001) and a contributor to architectural journals in Europe and North America.

Resumé

1984	Annette Gigon and Mike Guyer both graduated from the Federal Institute of Technology, Zurich (ETH).
1985–8	Annette Gigon worked for Herzog & de Meuron in Basel.
1984–7	Mike Guyer worked for OMA.
1987–9	Annette Gigon and Mike Guyer worked independently in their own architectural practices.
1989	Established joint architectural practice, Gigon/Guyer. Won first prize for the competition to design the Kirchner Museum, Davos.
1992	Completed the Vinikus Restaurant, Davos.
1994	Completed single family house for doctor's family in Canton of Zurich.
1995	Completed the extension to the Museum of Art, Winterthur.
1996	Completed the sports centre in Davos.
1998	Completed the renovation of Reinhart Collection, Römerholz, in Winterthur. Completed the Museum Liner Appenzell. Won first prize in a competition (in cooperation with Othmar Brügger) for a study commission for a street maintenance centre in Davos. Won first prize in the competition for an archaeological museum and park in Osnabrück, Germany. (Now in planning process.) Won first prize for a study commission Erweiterung und Erneuerung Appisberg, in Männedorf.
1999	Completed signal box in Zurich. Won first prize for study commission of the Pflegerinnenschule housing project in Zurich. (Planning process started.)
2000	Study commission completed for a housing project, Susenbergstrasse Zurich, in Zurich. Won first prize in the competition for the collection Albers/Honegger Mouans Sartoux, France. (Planning process started.)
2001	Residential housing in Kilchberg. Second stage. (Planning process started.)

Sendai Mediatheque

Jeremy Melvin describes how Toyo Ito used Le Corbusier's Maison Domino as a metaphoric starting point for an electronic-media centre in the city of Sendai in Japan. The result is a structure of the utmost sophistication and subtlety. It has a technologically advanced skin of glass and aluminium with optical devices to reflect the sun, as well as a columnar system of twisting tubes that unite structure and services together.

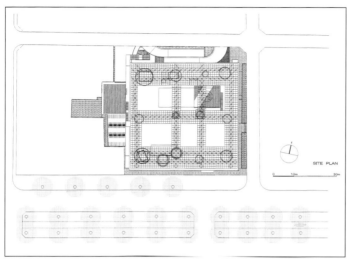

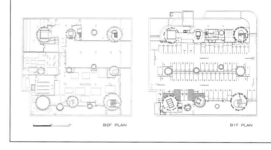

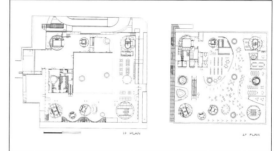

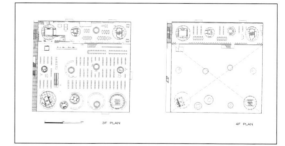

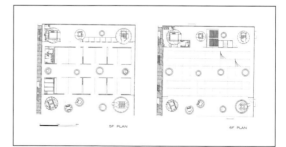

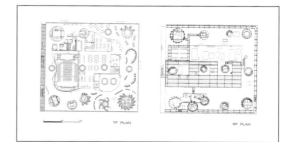

At the Sendai Mediatheque, Toyo Ito had an opportunity to bring his concept of 'blurring architecture' to fruition. For some time he had explored the idea that modern humans exist on two levels: the body as a physical entity subject to influences from nature; and the body as 'a flow of electrons', subject to stimuli from modern communication systems which might originate far beyond the body's sensory perception. In gizmo-laden, gadget-saturated Japanese society, where buildings are — or at least were until the economic downturn — fleeting will-o'-the wisps whose primary purpose might be to display messages, this duality is especially powerful. In buildings like the Tower of the Winds (1986), a ventilation tower to an underground shopping centre which wants to be a radio mast decorated for a festal circus, Ito had hinted at an architecture of ephemera which still served bodily needs. At Sendai, the programme called for a library, art gallery, visual image theatre and information centre. Here the body as receptor of electronic communication would overlap with its breathing, drinking and sense-perceiving physical analogue. It raises the dual dynamics of architecture's relationship to society, and the real to the virtual.

Sendai is a city of about one million people, some 500 kilometres north of Tokyo. A rise in service employment has not quite matched the decline of its traditional industries. In 1995 the city held a competition for a mediatheque on a city centre site, and it was completed in July 2000. Ito's design starts metaphorically with one of the classic images of modernism, Le Corbusier's Maison Domino, but updates it for an urban context in the 21st century. Conceptually a series of horizontal floor plates resting on a series of columns, its inspiration comes metaphorically from opening fibre-optic cables and injecting their contents into a traditional steel frame.

The city centre site means the mediatheque's footprint covers three-quarters of its 4,000-square-metre site, and it

Top left
Section through the tubes closest to the southern edge. The uses, finishes and heights of the floors differ, but the tubes are a constant presence albeit one that assumes a variety of characteristics.

Bottom left
Section through the central row of tubes. If the floors and the perimeter of the building conceptually belong to the world of human-made industrial machines, the tubes relate to an unusual combination of the elemental and psychological worlds. Air and energy are distributed through them, but so are visitors, each with their own desires and needs which the building might satisfy.

Top right
The interior of one of the tubes while under construction, at first-floor level. The tubes are made from thick-walled, slender steel pipes 120—140 millimetres in diameter. Used as a single layer truss, they make a structure which is both rigid and transparent suggesting that the dynamic of the information age has dispelled the mechanistic rigour of modernism. As each floor has a distinct character, the tubes, bearing people, information, air or energy, are reminders of the world outside.

Bottom right
The sixth floor before pouring the concrete. The almost square (50 x 49 metre) floor plates have a main structure of steel honeycomb slabs, 400 millimetres deep and 1,000-square-millimetres grid size. 70 millimetres of lightweight concrete makes the topping. This floor structure spans between the tubes, leaving an otherwise unimpeded horizontal zone. Different finishes, lighting, enclosures or other features give each floor its distinct character.

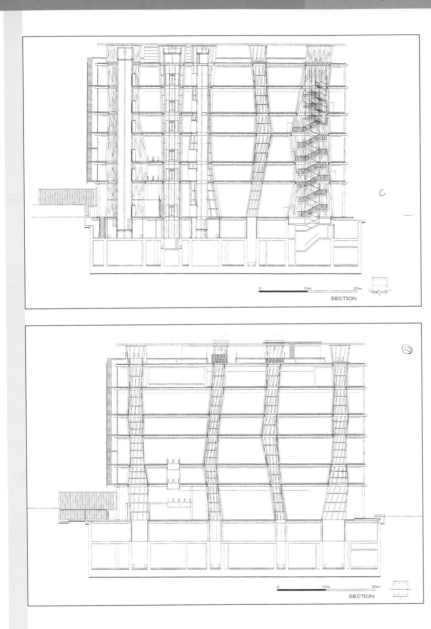

SECTION

SECTION

has eight floors plus two basements. Corbusier, interested in a purely structural rhetoric, ignored the need for enclosure. Ito's building has a sophisticated skin of glass and aluminium, double-layered on the south facade and capped by optical devices to reflect light into the heart of the 50-metre-square floor plates. The skin becomes a mediating device, adapting nature to the needs of the physical body. And despite Corbusier's interest in new technology — he even starred in a film about his villa at Garches — it was more to do with the representation of his buildings after their construction than the possibilities of transforming them during design. Ito's programme suggests new ways of interacting with information technology and other people, and its architecture seeks to express this potential for transformation. There is no need for a film about the mediatheque; it is undeniably a spectacle in its own right.

At Sendai, the columns are not single pieces of steel or concrete but twisting tubes. They twist and split: it is as if the hidden world of microwaves has shattered Corbusier's piloti, and imposed an order of its own. Within these 13 tubes are all the vertical circulation, elevators, air ducts, wiring and IT systems, and above two central ones are the roof-top louvres which reflect light down into the building. As well as combining the two aspects of the body, these tubes also unite structure and services, natural and artificial, poetic and prosaic. As a device they make visible those parts of a building which propriety often demands to be hidden, such as servicing, and attempts visual representation of what is naturally invisible, such as radio waves. They also suggest a parallax — a sense that no orthogonal frame can ever contain everything. And, varying in

Left
All three components — tubes, plates and skin — are distinctly identifiable in the completed building. The way the tubes pierce the floor plates indicates their status, not just as structure but also as the carriers of the technology that animates the building. Their unusual visual effect is reminiscent, perhaps, of depictions of electronic or radio waves in science fiction films. The floor plates are horizontal and only interrupted by the tubes, neutral bearers of whatever human activity is desired. The skin is physically the outermost part, but visually the most recessive reflecting its status as the necessary controller of the climate, assisting control of the internal environment, and as a barrier to noise.

Top right
The first spectacle — a test of the light performance in preparation for the opening ceremony. The complex geometry of the tubes creates an extraordinary series of effects which spread across the floors.

Bottom right
Ross Lovegrove's shelving on the seventh floor complements the curving form of the enclosure for the studio theatre. With the randomly placed lighting, this floor makes a contrast to the orthogonally placed shelves on the library levels, and the box-like enclosures of the gallery spaces.

shape from floor to floor, they question the artificial stability of modernism, suggesting instead stability at a deeper level, a dynamic, where the forces of the digital age are kept in equilibrium, if at all, in the perceptions of individuals.

Each of these three components — skin, tubes and floor plates — relates to some generic condition of architecture. The tubes relate to structure; the largely glass skin to enclosure. Occasional substitutions of glass for aluminium or cement panels reflect internal requirements, but the most significant adaptation of the standard modernist glass wall is the double-layered south facade, acting both as an acoustic barrier to a busy road and a buffer zone against solar gain. The plates are clear apart from the tubes and offer a version of universal space. Exploiting this, each floor holds information in a different way, or provides for a different means of communication between people.

The ground floor houses an 'open square', a 20-square metre space at the centre of the plan, as well as a restaurant and shop. Free-form, brightly coloured shapes contrast with the geometrical forms of the tubes and the Euclidian space of the plates. The public can come into the building as easily as they can walk across the square. And that means everyone. One floor up is the information centre for people of limited mobility, sight and hearing, with administrative offices and several other functions. Each is contained within a billowing curtain-like wall. Against these flowing shapes the perforated-steel louvre ceiling strongly expresses the grid. The library on the next two floors, and the gallery on the two above that, follow a more orthogonal layout. The bookcases in the library fit the grid within an otherwise open-plan space, while the

Below
Christmas 2000. With the tubes transformed into filigrees of light almost indistinguishable from the trees outside, the floors seem to float in space. Here the real and virtual worlds, the realms of information, imagination and sensory perception, melt into a seamless continuum.

All photos: Naoya Hatakeyama. Hatakeyama documented the construction process of the mediatheque. In capturing the unplanned and unfinished elements during construction, his photographs reveal much about the conceptual thinking as well as the intended outcome of the design. These photographs come from an exhibition held at the Architectural Association from 10 March to 28 April 2001.

gallery's lower floor has several enclosed spaces each of which is between 50 and 100 square metres. The upper floor is a single clear space which can be divided by movable partitions. One floor up, on the top public floor (there is a plant area above), is the 180-seat studio theatre contained within an island defined by a curving skin of glass and CD racks. Lights placed randomly in the ceiling add to the variety of effects.

These floors consciously exploit the large open floor plate of the base building to create a range of spatial effects. Differing floor-to-ceiling heights and different finishes on each surface reinforce their particular character. Each floor relates to a specific concept of architecture and might be suitable for definite functions. But the presence of the tubes is a constant reminder that none of these spatial orders is in itself

sufficient; another order always impinges. Although visitors may come for one specific activity they might be induced to sample another, and the underlying frame — both physical and conceptual — which unites these activities derives from an architectural sensibility.

The activities — performance, libraries and images — have the potential to transform themselves through new technology. By their nature they encourage introspection and self-criticism; they are never static. Ito turns the condition on the canon of modernist architecture to transform it into a perception of how cultural activities relate to each other and society in the digital age. ∆

Book Review

ON CERTAIN POSSIBILITIES FOR THE RADICAL EMBELLISHMENT OF A TOWN: Ten Urban Artefacts, by Eric Parry and Peter Carl, Black Dog Publishing, 2000, 96 pages, £14.95/$36.50.

This book novelly uses the architectural artefact as a vehicle for urban research to highlight student works from the Cambridge University Architecture programme. From the mobile appendages of the ubiquitous street-hustler to ergonomically responsive digital portals, the projects illustrate an architecture that is, at once, reactionary, appropriate, and street-wise.

Architect Eric Parry, and Historian, Peter Carl were correct when they wrote that the casual reader would likely place these works within the realm of art and lifestyle. Yet, as these works aspire to, and successfully achieve a high level of inventiveness, the focus for Parry lies less in their artistry than in tectonics and process. It is in the act of making, Parry maintains, that the distance between art and architecture is traversed.

Granted the text offers insight into the process of fabrication, the most appealing aspect is the story told not by Parry, but by the artefacts themselves. Made possible through an acute awareness of their context, the works are a first-generation progeny of their specific situations. 'The Leaner', (José Esteves de Matos) for example, a visibly public reconciliation of the miles of discomforting separation fencing in the streets of downtown London, responds to issues of territoriality and personal privacy. 'The Vendor's Box', (Peter Ferretto) whose primary criteria are lightness and transformability, is both a product and purveyor of transience in the urban continuum. Ultimately, these projects remind us to continually pay attention to our surroundings. With each artefact-inspired opportunity for spontaneous participation, we are reminded that the distinction between public and private is not always clear. Both in and of their context, these works thrive on the ambiguity of the borderline and successfully absorb the difference.

Responding to the formal and aesthetic complexities of modern city-space, *Ten Urban Artefacts* is, in a word, provocative. Speaking volumes in its 96 pages, the works are engaging, the text informative and the graphics vibrant. Far more than simply a collection of studio work, it celebrates the urban fabric as a medium for cultural interaction and experience, and highlights the often-overlooked objects that strive to make it so. ɷ *Sean Stanwick*

VAUGHAN OLIVER, VISCERAL PLEASURES, text by Rick Poynor, Booth-Clibborn Editions, 2001, 224 pages, £35.00

As a Part 3 student working next door to the London Palladium in the late 80s, I used to bunk off to HMV for as long as I could. One of my wishes at the time was that my favourite music, heavy metal, could have covers like Modern English, the Cocteau Twins, This Mortal Coil, Xmal Deutschland, The Pixies and the beautiful, almost Japanese, calligraphy of 'Sleeps with the Fishes' by Peter Hooten and Michael Brook. It never occurred to me that all these might be the work of one graphic designer. Doggedly, I stuck to the demons and wizards of metal covers. Only once did I buy a record — 'Earth Inferno' by Fields of the Nephilium, a Goth band— just for its cover.

Over 10 years later, when I convinced Maggie Toy at Wiley-Academy to publish my monograph *Maverick Deviations*, I searched out Chris Bigg, the graphic designer of the Nephilium album. Beggars Banquet told me he was part of an outfit called v23. A few days later I was sitting in v23's studio with Vaughan Oliver and Chris Bigg, being shown their portfolio, and showing them mine, and discovering the true extent of the Oliver oeuvre.

But back to the book. A comprehensive monograph of the work of Vaughan Oliver, it covers his work for the record company 4AD, his collaboration with Nigel Grierson, 23 Envelope, his work with Chris Bigg at v23 and has a commentary by design writer Rick Poynor. Vaughan was inspired by the Surrealists, particularly Dali, at college and later by the weird, strangely perverted photography of Joel-Peter Within. The book starts with a monkey in a Noddy hat and a plaster cast of Vaughan's teeth, so we know immediately that we're in business. Buy this book! In an era when the world and his wife think the computer gives them a mandate to be graphic designers, this book shows what a real graphic designer can do. The legacy of Vaughan's work is everywhere, seldom acknowledged, but a pervasive force in the history of graphic design in the 20th century. I look forward to being on the periphery as Vaughan and Chris make their mark on the 21st century as well. ɷ *Neil Spiller*

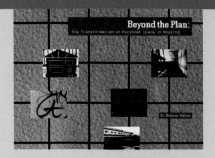

BEYOND THE PLAN
Stephen Willats
PB 0 471 50007 0; £19.99; 189 x 246 mm;
144 pages; September 2001

Since the early 1960s, artist Stephen Willats has been a proponent of the theory that the meaning of a work of art does not depend solely on the intention of the artist — that the idea of sole authorship is simply a symptom of our hierarchical culture. Art, he claims, is an interactive process involving the artist, the viewer and the society in which they exist. Likewise, the significance of a work of architecture is dependent not only upon the architect's vision, but also upon the lifestyles, attitudes and relationships of the people inhabiting it.

Within the apparent monotony of the endless streets of structurally-identical terraced houses that sprawl out from our cities, of the vast looming tower blocks that have dominated the skylines since the middle of the last century, and of the geometrically modularised inner-city estates, each unit is individualised by its occupants. *Beyond the Plan* is essentially a book about the way in which we transform our own personal space as an expression of ourselves whilst still dwelling within plans and room layouts imposed on us by architects.

The book centres around a series of works created by Willats between the late 1970s and the late 1990s in collaboration with people living on estates in London, Bath and Berlin. The related interviews are published here. They examine the personalisation of the dwelling space itself, both as a reinforcement of the resident's feelings of stability and as a sign of their identity to the outside world; the individualisation of the immediate environment; and the ways in which adjacent spaces such as wastelands and allotments are transformed into places of escape.

The interviewees, although sharing similar living conditions, express vastly varying personal viewpoints and experiences. The entire spectrum of ages is represented, from small children to the elderly. Their tastes and attitudes range from the conventional to the rebellious — from floral chintz and figurines to black leather and skulls. Despite this diversity, Willats has discovered a certain amount of common ground, and the interviews are complemented by essays explaining his findings.

Beyond the Plan will appeal to anyone with an interest in the sociological implications of architecture. This is a book which gives a voice to the inhabitants of buildings — who in the end play as significant a role in creating the identity of their dwellings as the architects themselves. *Ð*

SUSTAINABLE ECOSYSTEMS AND THE BUILT ENVIRONMENT
Guy Battle and Christopher McCarthy
PB 0 471 50007 0; £19.99; 305 x 252 mm; 112 pages; October 2001

As the world grows more and more densely populated, sustainability is becoming an ever more important concern in architecture. Architects are quite rightly being encouraged to take a more wide-ranging and considerate approach to their designs as they face challenges ranging from sick-building syndrome to global warming. New technologies are constantly being developed as a response to increasing awareness of the adverse effects that buildings can have on their environment and on those who live or work within them.

There can be few people who are as highly qualified to write on this area as Guy Battle and Christopher McCarthy of Battle McCarthy Consulting Engineers, who have many years' experience in green design and research. *Sustainable Ecosystems and the Built Environment* is a compilation of essays written by them for *Architectural Design* between 1994 and 1997, along with one new article published in the current issue.

The book covers the full range of issues concerned with sustainable architecture, emphasising the fact that truly sustainable design requires consideration not only of a building's occupants and immediate surroundings, but also of the wider effects it may have on the global ecosystem. Theories are backed up by practical examples, with cutting-edge green projects from all over the world presented in detail. Beginning with a history of the involvement of engineering with architecture — a collaboration which forms the basis of sustainable design — the book goes on to investigate building materials, wind engineering, energy sources, landscape design and urban planning principles. It also investigates the effects of buildings on their occupants, covering the air circulation, lighting and heating that is required for a healthy living/working environment and the ways in which colour and odour can influence mood.

It has never been more essential for architects, engineers and urban planners to be fully aware of the question of sustainability. This book is therefore invaluable, giving guidelines for professional practice and highlighting the potential of new technologies to increase and maintain the quality of life on this planet. *Ð*

Site Lines

M. Sean Stanwick describes how, with their new student residence for the Univerisity of Toronto, Morphosis and Stephen Teeple have succeeded in creating a gateway for the college and a landmark for the city.

Cities around the world long to bring home a signature building of recognized calibre, one that will assert their presence on the world cultural scene. One need only think of Bilbao to fully understand the impacts of landing a coveted work by Gehry, Koolhaas or Tschumi.

Graduate House, the recently completed graduate student residence at the University of Toronto is poised to be such a work. In winning the international open-competition, Thom Mayne of California's Morphosis, together with Toronto architect Stephen Teeple, have successfully rejuvenated a once proud yet often-neglected typology.

The first born of a campus-wide redevelopment initiative, the mandate was clear: a 'landmark' project to serve as a primary campus gateway. Programmatically the parti is quite simple as it is essentially a standard apartment block. It reads however, as four separate elements enclosing a sunken courtyard, a reflecting pool and terrace, all accessible from the sidewalk. Accommodations for 433 students are provided in three and four bedroom apartments arranged in combinations of single- and two-storey units with corridors on every third floor.

The façade, although tame by Mayne's own admission, is every bit a Morphosis event. Articulated in a manner never before seen in Canada, skins of charcoal-coloured concrete and perforated metal wrap and then retreat to expose the solids of the structure below. In doing so, Mayne has skilfully exploited an urban aesthetic through a series of richly layered, multivalent forms and spaces.

At the centre of the debate however, is what has become known as The Big O. Unlike the traditional vocabulary of the conventional framed gateway, the transparent band is simultaneously threshold, structure and sign. The O is actually the last letter in a giant illuminated marquee in which the words "University of Toronto" are ghosted onto green fritted glass. Challenging the terms of the historically accepted building-street relationship, the nervously cantilevered cornice is liberated from its site to freely intrude into the public space of the street. In a move specifically designed to challenge the pervasive public complacency, Teeple suggests the project was "about the fine line between the urbanistically responsible and something that...disturbs, that breaks through the responsible guideline." While Mayne sees the humour in the sign, the local opposition bewilders him as well. "This is the edge...it is a symbol of the university. What more appropriate place to demonstrate the power of architecture?"

Public opinion notwithstanding, the most salient quality of Graduate House is an acceptance of its metropolitan presence and responsibility. Transcending mere utility, it skilfully uses its form and siting to play a greater urban role than its programme dictates. Positioned at the crossroads of educational trends and public perceptions, it responds to, and ultimately celebrates the terms of the urban edge condition. A critical point of transition between civic and academic space, Graduate House is at once a physical and theoretical portal between living and learning; city and campus.

Historically, campus housing has a long history of academic servitude as a vital element in campus design. Too often however, it has found itself relegated to the role of background fabric. Here, Mayne and Teeple have restored the front-lines position of the residence typology and in doing so, re-established the necessary dialogue between building and context. In a gesture that would make Nolli proud, Graduate House delivers many of the essential elements necessary for the realization of a coherent urban ensemble including a sequential hierarchy of public and private spaces, and a filtering of events through direct interaction with the urban fabric.

An adage reads, "When the pupil is ready, the master will appear." The appropriate design corollary might well read, "When the city is ready, the building will appear." Rising to slay the dragon that is institutionalized form, it will revel as a signature piece that responds to the synergies of urban/academic life. Comprehensible as a whole, yet understood as a something more than the sum of its parts, Graduate House provides an interconnected atmosphere of exchange that spans urban and academic contexts. ⌀

Subscribe Now for 2001

As an influential and prestigious architectural publication, *Architectural Design* has an almost unrivalled reputation worldwide. Published bi-monthly, it successfully combines the currency and topicality of a newsstand journal with the editorial rigour and design qualities of a book. Consistently at the forefront of cultural thought and design since the 60s, it has time and again proved provocative and inspirational – inspiring theoretical, creative and technological advances. Prominent in the 80s for the part it played in Post-Modernism and then in Deconstruction, ⚛ has recently taken a pioneering role in the technological revolution of the 90s. With ground-breaking titles dealing with cyberspace and hypersurface architecture, it has pursued the conceptual and critical implications of high-end computer software and virtual realities. ⚛

⚛ Architectural Design

SUBSCRIPTION RATES 2001
Institutional Rate: UK £150
Personal Rate: UK £97
Discount Student* Rate: UK £70
OUTSIDE UK
Institutional Rate: US $225
Personal Rate: US $145
Student* Rate: US $105

*Proof of studentship will be required when placing an order. Prices reflect rates for a 2001 subscription and are subject to change without notice.

TO SUBSCRIBE
Phone your credit card order:
UK/Europe: +44 (0)1243 843 828
USA: +1 212 850 6645
Fax your credit card order to:
UK/Europe: +44 (0)1243 770 432
USA: +1 212 850 6021

Email your credit card order to:
cs-journals@wiley.co.uk
Post your credit card or cheque order to:

UK/Europe: John Wiley & Sons Ltd.
Journals Administration Department
1 Oldlands Way
Bognor Regis
West Sussex PO22 9SA
UK

USA: John Wiley & Sons Ltd.
Journals Administration Department
605 Third Avenue
New York, NY 10158
USA

Please include your postal delivery address with your order.

All ⚛ volumes are available individually. To place an order please write to:
John Wiley & Sons Ltd
Customer Services
1 Oldlands Way
Bognor Regis
West Sussex PO22 9SA

Please quote the ISBN number of the issue(s) you are ordering.

⚛ is available to purchase on both a subscription basis and as individual volumes

---

○ I wish to subscribe to ⚛ Architectural Design at the **Institutional rate of £150**.

○ I wish to subscribe to ⚛ Architectural Design at the **Personal rate of £97**.

○ I wish to subscribe to ⚛ Architectural Design at the **Student rate of £70**.

STARTING FROM ISSUE 1/2001.

○ Payment enclosed by Cheque/Money order/Drafts.

Value/Currency £/US$ ▭

○ Please charge £/US$ ▭ to my credit card.

Account number:

▭▭▭▭▭▭▭▭▭▭▭▭▭▭▭▭

Expiry date:

▭▭▭▭▭▭

Card: Visa/Amex/Mastercard/Eurocard *(delete as applicable)*

Cardholder's signature ▭
Cardholder's name ▭
Address ▭
▭
▭ Post/Zip Code ▭

Recepient's name ▭
Address ▭
▭
▭ Post/Zip Code ▭

I would like to buy the following Back Issues at £19.99 each:

○ ⚛ 152 Green *Architecture*, Brian Edwards

○ ⚛ 151 *New Babylonians*, Iain Borden + Sandy McCreery

○ ⚛ 150 *Architecture + Animation*, Bob Fear

○ ⚛ 149 *Young Blood*, Neil Spiller

○ ⚛ 148 *Fashion and Architecture*, Martin Pawley

○ ⚛ 147 *The Tragic in Architecture*, Richard Patterson

○ ⚛ 146 *The Transformable House*, Jonathan Bell and Sally Godwin

○ ⚛ 145 *Contemporary Processes in Architecture*, Ali Rahim

○ ⚛ 144 *Space Architecture*, Dr Rachel Armstrong

○ ⚛ 143 *Architecture and Film II*, Bob Fear

○ ⚛ 142 *Millennium Architecture*, Maggie Toy and Charles Jencks

○ ⚛ 141 *Hypersurface Architecture II*, Stephen Perrella

○ ⚛ 140 *Architecture of the Borderlands*, Teddy Cruz

○ ⚛ 139 *Minimal Architecture II*, Maggie Toy

○ ⚛ 138 *Sci-Fi Architecture*, Maggie Toy

○ ⚛ 137 *Des-Res Architecture*, Maggie Toy

○ ⚛ 136 *Cyberspace Architecture II*, Neil Spiller

○ ⚛ 135 *Ephemeral/Portable Architecture*, Robert Kronenburg

○ ⚛ 134 *The Everyday and Architecture*, Sarah Wigglesworth